CAMPING WITH KIDS IN THE WEST

Jayne Seagrave

CAMPING
WITH
KIDS
IN THE
WEST

BC and ALBERTA'S BEST
FAMILY CAMPGROUNDS

VICTORIA · VANCOUVER · CALGARY

Heritage House Publishing Company Ltd.
heritagehouse.ca

CATALOGUING INFORMATION AVAILABLE FROM LIBRARY AND ARCHIVES CANADA

978-1-77203-040-2 (pbk)
978-1-77203-041-9 (epub)
978-1-77203-042-6 (epdf)

Edited by Kate Scallion
Proofread by Judith Brand
Cover and book design by Jacqui Thomas
Cover photo by Mik122/iStockphoto.com. Interior photos courtesy of Jayne Seagrave unless otherwise credited.

The interior of this book was produced on 100% post-consumer recycled paper, processed chlorine free, and printed with vegetable-based inks.

Canadian Heritage Patrimoine canadien   The Canada Council for the Arts   Le Conseil des Arts du Canada   BRITISH COLUMBIA ARTS COUNCIL

Heritage House acknowledges the financial support for its publishing program from the Government of Canada through the Canada Book Fund (CBF), Canada Council for the Arts, and the Province of British Columbia through the British Columbia Arts Council and the Book Publishing Tax Credit.

19 18 17 16 15 1 2 3 4 5

Printed in Canada

→ Contents

→ Acknowledgements

t is difficult to remember, let alone list, the number of people who have been instrumental in assisting with the writing of this book and other camping books over the course of the last twenty years. This work has been researched and written with the help of an eclectic group of individuals that includes fellow campers, family, friends, park staff, and officials. While they remain nameless, these people have given me their time, experience, and knowledge during countless site visits, and through telephone calls and emails. I am indebted to all of them.

The excellent staff at Heritage House Publishing continue to offer support and expertise and have again proved a delight to work with. I am specifically grateful to Lara Kordic and Leslie Kenny for their guidance, insight, and time. In addition, Trevor Julier has supported this work with some excellent photographs and advice on campgrounds, adding to the quality of this text.

Finally, this book could not have been written had I not had the experience of family camping. My two sons, Jack Seaberry and Sam Seaberry, are now sixteen and fourteen, respectively, and have been camping all their lives. They have unwittingly shown me another side of camping, and have enabled me to appreciate the camping experience through eyes offering an alternative perspective. Their insights, enthusiasm, joie de vivre, and love for the outdoors has been a joy to watch develop. Their father, Andrew Dewberry, has been instrumental in developing the boys' passions and has consistently been supportive of them and me in all our bonding camping excursions. These three men have provided many fantastic memories and unforgettable experiences. They continue to amaze me with their actions, antics, and unorthodox activities. I could not have wished for better companions with whom to share my camping life.

→ Introduction

S ince January 8, 1999, my world has not been divided into black and white, rich and poor, old and young, fat and thin, but rather it has been split between those who do and those who do not have kids. For ten years, I camped in BC with only my spouse (and occasionally the province's mosquito population) for company. Since having children, there are times when I wonder if the mosquitoes would have been preferable to my two sons. As a parent, I know you are not supposed to readily acknowledge what a tsunami having children is, and how they radically influence every aspect of your life—but they do. And they do alter your camping life.

Over the course of the last sixteen years, I have taken my husband and two sons to over one hundred provincial parks in British Columbia, Yukon, and Alberta. Every summer, we have camped at Alice Lake (north of Vancouver) and much farther afield: our summers are not complete without a camping trip, be that for two days or three weeks. My offspring are now teenagers so "persuading" them to go camping is not as easy as it was when they were in elementary school. But it still happens, albeit with a few concessions, which often involve finding Wi-Fi, taking additional teenage boys, and allowing them more freedom to wander and explore without parental supervision. These concessions are a small price to pay to get them outside into the wonderful Canadian countryside.

This book includes what I believe to be some of the best family-oriented campgrounds in British Columbia and Alberta in both national and provincial parks. Over ten years ago, I wrote another book about family camping, drawing heavily on my personal experiences taking preschoolers camping in BC campgrounds. This book includes information on fifteen BC campgrounds and ten Alberta campgrounds, and addresses the challenges and benefits of taking kids of *every* age camping. All of these campgrounds accept reservations. Most offer water-based activities and are close to population centres with medical services, fast food restaurants, and Wi-Fi links—yet are still far enough away to foster that get-away-from-it-all experience.

During much of the year, our time as parents is committed to school or daycare, and piano, swimming, soccer, or hockey lessons. Evenings and weekends are usually consumed with just the basics of preparing meals, cleaning, running errands, and supervising homework. As our children get older, the demands of exams and sports tournaments become even more pressing and the amount of time they spend in front of a computer, cellphone, tablet, or other device increases. Camping is a wonderful, economical way to enjoy your children in a different and stimulating environment. There are fantastic bonuses in travelling with your offspring to unknown destinations, living outside, sleeping under the stars, and in sharing their enthusiasm when experiencing the country from a totally new perspective.

Children who spend time in different locations expand their awareness of the world, and they bring an energy and exuberance to new experiences. They have no social barriers, and make friends easily and quickly. I believe camping is a gorgeous way to escape the city, meet others, learn about the outdoors, gain confidence, and have an adventure. Children will often remember their camping experience for the rest of their lives. I have found no two camping trips are ever the same, even if you do return to the same place. Each camping

The boys, all packed up and ready to go camping—a family tradition for as long as they can remember.

adventure is unique. It is why I love it, and why I have written this book: to encourage others to follow this path.

FAMILY CAMPING

What you can and cannot do when camping with kids depends on the age of your offspring, as each age brings unique experiences, joys, and challenges. Babies are portable and can be nicely packed away, but can crawl into everything if left on their own. Preschoolers don't have the stamina for long hikes, but at least they are out of diapers, making many other activities far more convenient. Teenagers can be taken on long canoe trips and hikes, but sometimes need to be bribed with promises of cellphone and Wi-Fi connections before they agree to this type of holiday.

How time flies! The boys as toddlers, deciding what to pack for a camping trip.

Camping While Pregnant

Strangely enough, few books on pregnancy touch on the topic of camping while pregnant. Each woman experiences pregnancy differently: some breeze through it while others have a hell of a time. I had many good nights sleeping in a tent when I was eight months pregnant and would say that if you're feeling up to it, do it.

The only problem I had camping while I was pregnant was the number of bathroom trips I had to make in the middle of the night, which meant squatting while balancing an extra 30 pounds in front. Toppling over and trying to right yourself, semi-naked in the dark at 2:00 a.m. does make you realize why heavily pregnant women may wish to think twice about camping, or at least opt for the campsite nearest to the toilet. Remember also to pack plenty of pillows to support the bump if you're sleeping in a tent.

Camping with Babies or Toddlers

If your baby is not yet a crawler, camping is easy. Okay, you do have to take more stuff, but you can leave the baby happily goo-gooing in the car seat on the picnic table while you pitch the tent. A playpen can be used as a crib, and a mosquito net can be easily laid over the top, should bugs be a problem.

Camping with toddlers, however, is another matter. This age can be the most challenging because of all the equipment they require, their need for diapers, and their propensity to put everything in their mouths. The great outdoors, replete with animals, rocks, stones, water, dirt, vegetation, and insects, can't be childproofed as easily as your home. I believe the secret to camping with toddlers is to be relaxed about it. So they don't have a wash before going to bed, or they sleep in the clothes they've been in all day, or they delight in treading on the ants and poking the banana slugs with pinecones; let them do it. The biggest problem I found while tent camping with toddlers was in their early-morning waking. The dawn arrives, and their excitement over seeing you sleeping next to them stimulates their delight and curiosity; so you get up at 5:30 a.m. and experience the campground at a time few others will. Afternoon naps may also be a challenge if you try to get them to sleep in the unfamiliar tent. A better option is a gentle push in the stroller around the campground's roads, especially if these are gravel—an almost surefire way to send them to sleep.

Most of the difficulties of this tent-based experience are, of course, avoided by camping in a recreational vehicle (RV) camper, tent trailer, or towing trailer. If there is ever a time when you get rid of the tent and choose an RV, it is at this age (see *How to Camp* on page 17). On the plus side, kids of this age are still quite portable, so you can hike with them in a backpack—something that is not an option with preschoolers.

Camping with Preschoolers

While you can't send these young ones off to explore the campground on their own, children at this age are wonderful to take camping. The under-fives can actively get involved with camping and what it means to set up an outdoors home away from the urban centre. They can help select flat ground to put up the tent, get sticks for toasting marshmallows, explore adjacent undergrowth without eating it, take a ride on the tricycle, and run around and make noise. Expect them to stay up late, get dirty, make friends with the kids from the next campsite, play the best imaginary games, and have a ball.

Camping with this age group also means you can vacation in May, June, or September and avoid the crowds and the added expense of peak summer months. Make the most of it and remember to teach them your campsite number upon arrival, as well as basic safety information (see *Camping Safely* on page 16). Also remember to pack fishing nets, water shoes, and toys.

Camping with Preteens

By following a few simple rules, children this age will learn to love the camping experience. Provincial and national parks provide wonderful safe environments for children to explore by themselves. Parents do not have to worry about unsafe roads and fast drivers, video arcades, or TV. Children can gain some independence by learning and exploring safely on their own. Parks are fantastic for cycling, rollerblading, swimming, and exploring with new-found friends or with friends brought from home. Remember their board games, crayons, sidewalk chalk, balls, bikes, rollerblades, and books, and they will be sure to entertain themselves. The big disadvantage for this age group is the restriction of having to camp during school holidays and weekends, when parks are most crowded. A little planning ahead helps a lot, though; these are the times when you really appreciate the reservation system (see *Reservations* on page 27).

Camping with Teenagers

Let me first admit and acknowledge that teenagers can be a challenge in *any* environment, so for many parents, the idea of taking a reluctant, emotional adolescent away for a week's camping trip is comparable to having a root canal without anaesthetic. While teenagers can be obnoxious, self-absorbed, arrogant, and moody, at least if they display these traits at home, there is another room for the rest of the family to hide in. Escaping this is not so easy in the great outdoors. For many parents, taking teenagers on a camping trip may be one step too far. But for those of us who are willing to override the objections, there are a number of benefits, and if you are prepared to host one of their friends, many of these issues can be curtailed.

In 2013, despite countless protests, I took our family on a three-week trip to the Yukon. As a family, we listened to numerous books on the stereo during the long car journeys, each one of us taking a turn deciding what we should listen to. When we got to our campsite, the boys took complete responsibility for erecting their own tent and getting their beds made. They chose the location of the camping spot,

As children grow, family camping takes on a different—but still fun!—dynamic.

collected wood and water, made fires, cooked dinner each night (as they had no desire to wash up and the deal was whoever cooked did not have to wash up), decided what food we should buy, explored the campgrounds independently, and advised on the activities for each day. Our long camping excursion was broken up every third to fourth day by a night in a motel and dinner in a restaurant of their choice. The trip was a wonderful bonding experience, punctuated with activities they wanted to do (whitewater rafting, eating at Boston Pizza, locating the only Internet cafe with Wi-Fi and remaining there for two hours so they could reconnect with friends). Camping with teenagers involves not only including them as equal partners, but also becoming involved in activities you may not want to do to keep them happy, forgetting the rules that are enforced at home (like regular washing, changing clothes, and curfew), and introducing them and appreciating them within environments they rarely see.

CAMPING SAFELY

When you arrive at a campground, remember to teach your children to memorize the campsite number. A few years ago, BC Parks and the Royal Canadian Mounted Police (RCMP) offered guidelines on what children should know while in the woods through the Hug a Tree program, which started in San Diego and was subsequently adopted across North America. Here are some highlights from this program.

Hug a Tree and Survive

1 Tell your parents where you are going, with whom, and when you plan to return.
2 Stay on well-marked trails and always hike with a buddy.
3 Wear brightly coloured, warm clothing, and bring a hat.
4 Carry a garbage bag and whistle (a garbage bag can be used to keep you warm if you get lost, and a whistle attracts attention and can be heard from farther away than a voice).
5 Carry a non-perishable snack and drink.

6 If you get lost, hug a tree—it can help you feel better and offers shelter. It will also keep you in one place so you have a better chance of being found.

7 Help people find you. Don't hide if you see someone looking for you.

8 Stay calm. You will feel safest and stay calm if you stay in one place. If you hear a noise that frightens you, yell out your name—animals tend to be more scared of you than you are of them.

9 Make yourself big. Try to pick a tree near a clearing so you can be easily seen.

HOW TO CAMP

RV, Tent, or Motel?

In spite of having a two-and-a-half-year-old and a nine-month-old, being constantly stressed and exhausted, and reaching my fortieth year, I believed I'd found my true nirvana in July 2001: a 24-foot GO WEST rented motorhome. Okay, some women dream of diamonds, others of BMW convertibles, and more wish for spouses who do not spend forty minutes in the bathroom at one time, but for me, life could not

Jack, ready to build a fire.

Sam heading into the RV.

have improved a bit from the moment I sat in those brown, heavily cushioned velour seats of my first rented RV. Camping would never be the same again. I had reached middle age, and if accepting middle age meant being comfortable in my watertight, warm, and air-conditioned RV, then so be it.

I had camped in a tent the previous year with my eighteen-month-old son, while I was eight months pregnant. Camping was a challenge. A year later, we took our motorized home to Alice Lake Provincial Park, to Lillooet, and then back down Highway 1 to Vancouver. The kids sat opposite each other in raised seats at the back of the camper, totally contented. Music could be played directly to them, and we were free to enjoy the scenery without listening to Raffi for the millionth time. There was a fridge, microwave, two large double beds with sheets and duvets, a toilet and shower, even space for the playpen. The disadvantage? A night in an RV during the high season cost the same as a night in a four-star Whistler hotel.

Recreational vehicles are not cheap to rent (or purchase and maintain), especially during the peak months of July and August. They do make the camping experience with kids a lot easier and just as enjoyable, and there are some good deals to be had if you go during the shoulder months of May, June, or September, or if there are enough adults to share the expense. (Remember, there is nothing to stop the adults from sleeping inside and letting older children camp under canvas outside.) When my children were toddlers, I really appreciated the darkness the RV offered (no waking at 5:00 a.m. with the dawn birds as they had done in a tent), the confinement of the loud crying fits (fellow campers also appreciated this), the fridge for keeping milk cool or the microwave for warming food, and the instant afternoon nap on the road, which we all were able to enjoy. If you can afford it, camping in an RV when your children are under three is highly recommended.

Camping obviously requires more than just a tent, and all the extra equipment can be costly, depending on what you decide you need. (I cover the basics in *What to Take Camping*—see page 20.) If you have never camped before and do not want to invest in all the gear only to find you are definitely not a camper, consider one of two options. Option one is to borrow the tent and gear from a friend. I would like to say that nothing much can go wrong with borrowing equipment, except that we loaned our tent and self-inflating mattresses to some novice campers a few years ago, and while they were asleep, their small dog, who was also in the tent, started to bark. To discover why the dog was excited they unzipped the tent only to find a skunk outside, which then proceeded to do what skunks do best—spray the tent. Our tent spent the next week soaking in tomato juice in an effort to get rid of the damage. The other option is to rent equipment. Mountain Equipment Co-op rents tents, mattresses, sleeping bags, and even kid carriers. It also offers a weekend special from 3:00 p.m. Thursday until 1:00 p.m. Monday when you pay for only two days, so you can see whether you and your family are indeed camping material.

Finally, I have to add that there is nothing wrong with deciding you (or your spouse or offspring) are not always the camping types and opting to stay in a lodge or motel. For example, I have camped at Alice Lake, but have also enjoyed this park as a day visitor and stayed at a motel in nearby Squamish, which has an excellent kids' waterslide and pool. Likewise, I have enjoyed camping at Manning Provincial Park for two nights and then spent the third night in the park's lodge.

Many of the stresses of camping (or of just being in constant close confines with your nearest and dearest) can be relieved by spending a night in a motel complete with air conditioning, TV, temperature-controlled showers, kitchens, laundry, and, of course, a soft bed. There is nothing wrong with combining camping and motel stays, and organizing your holiday to incorporate both. Regardless of your lodgings, there are some wonderful provincial and national parks to experience with your children, even if you do not camp in them.

Each camper has his or her own idea of the camping essentials. Even if you think you've covered every eventuality, this thought is probably naive. I don't think I've been on a camping trip when I haven't forgotten something, but that's part of the fun.

As our boys grew older, we invested in a two-dome tent with an interlocking connection. This tent effectively has two rooms, both with a separate entrance. Each dome can be erected separately, but also connected to the other to form two adjoining spaces—ideal when camping with young children who you may want to see easily. When shopping for a tent, check out what Canadian Tire has to offer. This store offers a great range of products for family camping.

My family sleeps on self-inflating mattresses that roll up tightly and are easy to pack, but which also provide a good night's sleep. Our children sleep in full-sized sleeping bags (which they find great fun, calling them "slug-sacks"), but we still prefer to pack up our duvet and sheets for a good night's rest. If you put young children in full-sized sleeping bags, you may want to include extra blankets (fleece is ideal) as they do tend to move out of the bags.

After twenty-five years of camping, I've found the best way to store and transport my camping gear is in large plastic containers: one for cooking utensils and crockery, one for our mattresses, one for food (non-perishable), and one for other stuff (flashlights, hibachi, foil, axe, insect repellent, tarps, matches, etc.). We also take a large cooler and a camp stove. The first time you camp, you'll take too much and forget all the important things, but with more experience, you'll get better at knowing what to take and what you don't need. Remember, in most cases, you can buy whatever you need as you travel.

Eating outside is a wonderful experience and, of course, just being outside makes you hungry. We purchase enough food for about three days, because after this time, even with the best cooler, fresh food tends to get a little ripe. Our staples are the clichéd hot dogs and marshmallows, supplemented by sweet corn, fresh vegetables and dips, and

Packing for Kids

- baby change pad
- beach tent (for shade)
- books
- bug collection kit (often available at dollar stores)
- compass
- crayons, pencils, paper
- fishing nets (Our family uses these to catch "toe-biters"—my father's name for small fry.)
- fishing rods
- flashlight or headlamp (good for late-night reading or trips to the washroom)
- games (e.g., balls, boules, Lego blocks, or equipment for field games)
- iPod, CDs, DVDs, or audio books for long car journeys
- life jackets
- magnifying glass
- playing cards
- sand toys (stored in a string bag so the sand falls away between visits to the beach)
- sidewalk chalk
- water shoes

Also Remember:

- aluminum foil
- axe
- backpack
- barbecue, hibachi, gas stove, and gas
- bowl for washing dishes
- bungee cords
- camera
- candles and lantern
- first-aid kit, including calamine lotion, bug spray, and sunscreen
- flashlights
- food
- funnel to collect water
- garbage bags/plastic bags (lots of spare ones if your kids are in diapers)
- maps
- matches and newspaper
- paper towels and wet wipes
- plastic containers for food
- pots, dishes, and cutlery
- rope
- sleeping bags and mattresses
- sunglasses and hats
- Swiss Army knife
- tarps
- tent
- tissues
- toiletries
- towels
- water container

fruit. We also have pita pockets, tortilla wraps, pasta, crackers, cheese, bacon, cereal, granola bars, and fruit bars. Other necessities include milk, juices, water, and the odd beer to keep the chefs hydrated. Boxes of wine also travel well. I always include non-perishables such as tins of pasta, tuna, and baked beans, and copious quantities of ketchup.

We often eat breakfast out because the children tend to wake up early. Many of the provincial park campgrounds have breakfast restaurants, or coffee bars serving baked goodies, within a 10-kilometre drive.

WHAT TO EXPECT AT A PROVINCIAL OR NATIONAL CAMPGROUND

National and provincial park campgrounds are well signposted on major highways. The first warning campers receive is a sign posted 2 kilometres before the campground turnoff, and another sign 400 metres from

Located near provincial park entrances, these information boards provide a map of the campground and warnings about area hazards.

the campground. The second sign gives directions to the access road. If a campground is full or closed, the park operator will post notices on these roadside signs stating this fact.

If you have a reservation at a campground (see *Reservations* on page 27), your reserved site will be listed at the park entrance. For those without a reservation, the biggest thrill upon arrival at a campground is deciding which spot to settle in. Occasionally, in some of the larger provincial campgrounds, parks staff pre-selects the sites. Depending on the season, time of day, and location of the park, your choice of spaces could be limited. Some parks have areas specifically designated for tents, while most provincial and national parks have spots suitable for either RVs or tents. A number of parks offer double spots, ideal for two families camping together, and pull-through spots for the larger RVs. There is usually a map of the campground at the entrance detailing where these spots are to be found.

Once you have established which sites are restricted, you will need to cruise the campground so you can pick a spot. Campsites by a beach, lake, river, or creek are most desirable, so head for these first. Avoid areas of stagnant water (mosquito breeding grounds) or sites next to the "thunderboxes" (pit toilets), which may exude unpleasant odours, attract flies, and disturb you with the noise of banging doors. Sites near the flush toilets and showers may seem convenient, especially if you are pregnant or have young children, but the downside is that between 5:00 p.m. and 11:00 p.m. and again from 7:00 a.m. to 11:00 a.m., most people at the campground will be visiting these facilities and walking past your site in order to get there.

As you drive around the campground, make note of your preferences and then claim your most desirable spot by parking a vehicle there. Alternatively, leave some item, such as a water jug or a plastic tablecloth, on the picnic table to state to the world that this spot is taken.

When you are established in your new home, you are ready to explore the campground. Remember to tell your children the campsite number and, if possible, a reference point (e.g., near the big tree, just by the amphitheatre). Your first stop should be a return to the information board at the campground entrance, as this will have a full map of the campground, details of any hazards in the area, information about other campgrounds in the region, and, if you're lucky, leaflets and maps.

You will want to familiarize yourself and your kids with the facilities available at the campground. All provincial and national park campgrounds included in this book have the basics: flush toilets, water, wood (for sale), pit toilets, picnic tables, and firepits. Larger campgrounds might have showers, baby-change facilities, sani-stations, wheelchair access, visitor centres, small stores, laundry (Alberta only), and group camping. Washroom facilities are generally well-maintained and clean. Gravel camping spots are tidied and raked after each visitor departs; garbage is regularly collected, and there are bins for recycling.

A park attendant collects fees (cash only) during the early evening hours and sells firewood. As you might expect, camping fees vary depending on the facilities provided; campgrounds with showers and electricity tend to be the most expensive while less-developed campgrounds have lower fees. At the time of writing, fees ranged from thirteen dollars to thirty-five dollars a day for BC provincial parks and up to thirty-two dollars for national parks (GST included). Alberta parks can charge as much as forty-four dollars per night for a site with all services. Firewood costs between seven and nine dollars. You can stay for as many nights as you want, up to a maximum of fourteen nights in both provincial and national parks. The attendant will post a receipt at your spot that displays the date you intend to leave.

The park attendants who collect fees are good sources of information on weather conditions, local activities, the best fishing locations, and so on. They also tend to be interesting characters, attributable, perhaps, to the long periods of time they have been working outdoors.

Washrooms/showers

The biggest reason people resist camping is undoubtedly because of the rougher washroom facilities. Having spent the first thirty years of my life in Europe, where finding toilet tissue in the washroom of a downtown pub after 8:00 p.m. is a luxury, I am amazed by the notion some people have that BC and Alberta Parks washroom facilities are unpleasant. Granted, a pit toilet in a popular provincial park in the heat of July is not a good place to read your favourite novel, but in spite of the slightly unpleasant odours and the flies, it will have been cleaned within the last twelve hours, so there will be plenty of toilet tissue.

There are basically three types of toilets in provincial and national parks. The first are the pit toilets—thunderboxes—boxes painted white inside, centrally located in various sections of the campground. The second type of toilet looks like a thunderbox but houses an odour-free flushing toilet. The third type is the conventional washroom with sinks; some of them contain showers. Park staff clean and service all three types of facilities twice daily.

The larger washrooms have mirrors that almost without exception give a distorted, unclear image, so do not expect to be able to apply makeup in front of one. The water temperatures in some campground showers may be a bit erratic, but they are generally adequate, and, unlike those in many private campgrounds, do not cut off after you have had the allotted two minutes and still have shampoo in your hair. Some campgrounds have family shower rooms and, increasingly, baby-change facilities—but don't expect these.

Water is available either from a conventional water faucet or from a pump. Collecting water from a pump is a bit of an art (expect to get wet feet, but to delight your children), and, in certain parks, the pumps will give your arm muscles a good workout. You may want to include a funnel with your camping gear, as it can help considerably when you are collecting pump water.

Garbage/recycling

You can tell if a campground is in an area inhabited by bears by the look of the garbage bins. If they are swinging barrels or elongated metal cylinders with tight lids and a catch, you can be sure there are bears around. Provincial and national parks do recycle, although the extent of recycling varies between parks. Remember that you should never leave garbage at your campsite, as it attracts racoons, chipmunks, skunks, crows, and even bears.

A note on bears: BC is bear country, with a quarter of the black bear and half of the grizzly bear population in Canada. Campers should never approach or feed bears. Food-conditioned bears—those that scavenge food from garbage cans and picnic tables—begin to associate food with people, lose their natural fear of humans, and become a threat to campers and to themselves. If bears are in the area, a notice to this effect will be on the campground notice board.

Recreational Activities

Activities offered at the park will vary, of course, depending on the size and location of it. Many parks have boat launches, safe swimming areas cordoned off for children (but have no lifeguards), hiking trails, adventure playgrounds, horseshoe pits, volleyball nets, large grassy areas for ball games, and amphitheatres. Interpretive programs are offered in larger parks during the peak summer months, and sometimes programs specifically designed for children are offered.

Parks Staff

Parks workers are usually delightful characters with unique personalities and idiosyncrasies. As the people responsible for these "huge, open-air hotels," their job is to keep the washrooms clean and tidy, garbage cleared, and campsites clean; to collect fees; and, of course, to ensure we all remain happy campers. What a lovely task. They wear blue shirts and shorts or trousers (brown in national parks), and are frequently an unbeatable source of information about the surrounding areas. They can also be useful in helping the novice camper light a campfire or suggesting the best place to pitch a tent.

Reservations

One of the biggest camping success stories is the reservation system. It allows campers to reserve spots at the more popular provincial and national parks. All of the campgrounds detailed in this book accept reservations.

The advantage of reservations is that they ensure accommodation for the night. For those with children, or with commitments that prevent an early getaway for a camping weekend, the reservation system does away with uncertainty and guarantees the joy of camping is not denied.

To make a reservation in BC, you can go online to discovercamping.ca or phone the Discover Camping Campground Reservation Service at 1-800-689-9025 between 7:00 a.m. and 7:00 p.m. (Pacific Time), Monday to Friday, and between 9:00 a.m. and 5:00 p.m. on Saturday and Sunday. This service is available from March 1 to September 15. At the time of writing, the fee to reserve was six dollars per night to a maximum of eighteen dollars for three to fourteen nights. This fee is subject to GST. Campers pay the reservation and campsite fees by credit card when making the reservation. You can reserve a site up to three months in advance, but a reservation must be made at least two days prior to your arrival at the campsite. You can cancel a reservation via voicemail or the Internet twenty-four hours a day.

If you do not have a reservation, campsites are available on a first-come, first-served basis. When you arrive at a campground, a notice board at the gate will provide details on which spots are reserved. Often it is possible to camp for one night at a spot that has not been reserved, but you need to check the notice board upon arrival to determine which sites these are.

The reservation system in Alberta is similar to that in BC. To reserve a campsite in Alberta, visit Reserve.AlbertaParks.ca or call 1-877-537-2757. The fee is twelve dollars per reserved campsite; therefore, reserving a space just for one night in a variety of campgrounds can be expensive. Reservations can be made up to ninety days prior to arrival with the maximum period being for sixteen nights.

Reservations at national park campgrounds can be made at: reservation.pc.gc.ca or by calling 1-877-737-3783. A fee of eleven dollars is taken per site reservation, in addition to the camping fee and the park entrance fee.

Staying Connected

Cellphone coverage across Canada is increasing: areas that six months ago had no coverage are now being connected. It is a constantly changing, dynamic situation. If access to your phone is vital during a camping trip, my advice would be to consult your cellphone provider to obtain a map of their coverage. I have found that while travelling across Canada, service fluctuates and often depends on how near you are to a core population. The best time to stay connected is usually when stopped to fill up on gas or coffee.

In 2014, national parks across Canada boasted the introduction of Wi-Fi service. It is important to remember this service is restricted to the area around the visitor centre and may not be available in the campground itself, which is frequently located away from this building. There is rarely service in other areas of these vast parks. The availability of Wi-Fi in BC and Alberta provincial parks is haphazard. Larger campgrounds with visitor centres usually have Wi-Fi and often have free Internet and access to computers in their buildings; however, farther afield and in the smaller remoter provincial parks, there is no connection. A word of warning: in my experience, these services offered by the larger campgrounds are often down, so should not be relied upon. We tend not to depend on any provision in the parks but rather ensure we stop at restaurants while on the road as they have free, reliable service and therefore limit our (and the kids') time on mobile devices.

POTENTIAL HAZARDS

At the entrance to each campground, you will find a list detailing any hazards in the campground. Here are some common hazards, including ones particularly dangerous for children.

Swimmer's Itch

Parasites living in freshwater snails and waterfowl can cause swimmer's itch, or *cercarial dermatitis*, a temporary skin irritation caused by the parasite's larvae entering the skin. The larvae thrive close to shore in the warm waters of lakes and ponds, often where Canada geese and other fowl are found. Because children go in and out of the water often and have tender skin, they are particularly vulnerable. Swimmer's itch can be avoided by applying skin oil (baby oil is a good choice) before swimming, towelling off briskly, and showering after swimming. Swimmer's itch develops as small red spots that can develop into blisters. Although unpleasant, the symptoms can be treated with calamine lotion and the condition usually clears up by itself within a week.

Poison Ivy

This low, glossy plant with three green leaves and white berries can produce severe skin rashes. It is prevalent on Vancouver Island and in the Okanagan. Calamine lotion is an effective treatment.

Sunburn

By its very nature, camping means being outdoors from sunrise to sunset, so make sure your children wear a hat and are protected by sunscreen. Special UV-protected swimwear is available that covers the whole body—an expensive but effective option. If you're near water, reapply sunscreen often. Remember that water reflects the sun's rays and can compound the sun's effect on skin. Increase exposure to the sun gradually, and remember to keep well hydrated.

Water

BC and Alberta parks do not have lifeguards, so keep a watchful eye on young children. Some parks have designated shallow swimming areas; others do not. It is the parents' responsibility to ensure their children's safety around water. When boating, you are required by law to carry properly fitting life jackets, or, for infants weighing between 10 and 15 kilograms, personal flotation devices (PFDs), which are worn more like a vest, have more flexibility, and are designed for situations where the swimmer can be rescued quickly. Many parents purchase a PFD specifically for their child's play near water; good ones should have a label showing the Canadian Coast Guard approval and weight guidelines. When non-swimmers play in or near water, it's good to establish rules; for example, they can go into the water only up to their chest, or stay within calling distance of you.

Bears

BC has almost one-quarter of all the black bears in Canada and about half of the grizzlies. Although people-to-bear encounters are extremely rare, campers should always remember they are in bear country. Generally, bears go out of their way to avoid people, but all bears are dangerous, and those with young cubs are especially so.

Anyone planning to enjoy the outdoors should learn how to recognize a black bear or grizzly bear, and how to respond accordingly. Black bears can be black, brown, cinnamon, or blond with short, curved claws, and a small shoulder lump. Grizzly bears can also be black, brown, or blond, are bigger than black bears, have long, curved claws, and a prominent shoulder hump. If walking in bear country, watch out for warning signs such as overturned rocks, bear scat, clawed trees, and chewed roots. Talk loudly, wear bear bells, or sing to make your presence known. If you encounter a bear at close range, avoid eye contact, move away slowly, and stay calm. If the bear approaches standing up, it is trying to identify you. Talk quietly so it knows you are human.

If it is lowering its head, snapping its jaws, and snorting, it is displaying aggression. This is serious. Do not run but continue to back away. If a grizzly shows aggression, consider climbing a tree. Generally the key is to not do anything to threaten or arouse the animal. If a grizzly attacks, play dead by adopting a tight, curled-up position with your head on your knees and your hands behind your head. Do not move until the bear leaves the area. If a black bear attacks, try to retreat; if this is not possible, fight back with rocks, sticks, and branches to deter the animal.

Never approach or feed bears. Food-conditioned bears begin to associate food with people and lose their natural fear of humans, becoming a threat to campers and themselves. With caution and sensible behaviour, you can safely camp and enjoy bear country.

Bugs

I have found bugs to be far more common in Alberta and the northern parts of BC than in the Okanagan, Lower Mainland, and on Vancouver Island, which is something to bear in mind when planning a trip. The most effective way to keep the mosquitoes and blackflies at bay is DEET, but it can be irritating to children and should not be used on babies under six months old. The Canadian Paediatric Society suggests children between six months and twelve years of age use repellent containing no more than 10 percent DEET. This solution provides three hours of protection. Soybean oil has also been found to be an effective, non-chemical repellent and was recently sanctioned by Health Canada. Mosquito nets for strollers are available from good camping stores and Canadian Tire.

Fire

Children should be taught to keep well away from the firepit and that it can remain hot even when the fire has gone out. Toddlers especially need to be watched closely if you are using the firepit.

Camping Tips

One of the joys of camping is learning the little tricks that make it easier. Here are a few tips:

1. If you do not have a reservation, try to arrive at a campground before 5:00 p.m., as the busiest hours for arrival are between 5:00 p.m. and 8:00 p.m.

2. If the campground does not have a shower, leave a full plastic water container in the sun all day long and wash in warm water in the evening.

3. Take a water container and a funnel to collect water from the pump.

4. Use bungee cords hooked between trees as clotheslines.

5. Cook vegetables (e.g., mushrooms, tomatoes, zucchini, peppers, and onions) by wrapping them in aluminum foil, sealing them in with spices.

6. It's a good idea to keep a key-ring-sized flashlight in your pocket for emergencies and for nightly excursions to the washroom.

7. Axes, matches, dry paper, plastic bags, rope, flashlights, candles, and aluminum foil are all camping basics.

8. Spread a tarp under the tent for extra protection against the damp.

9. Keep one set of clothes specifically for wearing by the campfire so you have only one outfit smelling of woodsmoke.

10. Dry wet wood by propping logs against the firepit.

11. Take folding chairs as they are far more comfy to sit in. (If you're breastfeeding, these chairs are a must.)

Now you are ready for a camping adventure . . . *GO FOR IT!*

HOW TO USE THIS BOOK

This book has been divided into five parts. Following this introductory chapter, Part 1 describes campgrounds in the most populated areas of BC: the Lower Mainland, Vancouver Island, and the Gulf Islands. Part 2 details campgrounds in the Shuswap/Okanagan region and the Rockies. The final two parts describe campgrounds in western and eastern Alberta. No privately owned campgrounds are included in this book. Although there are many privately run facilities perfect for family camping, my expertise is in government-owned (provincial and national) parks.

Each campground entry contains a number of subheadings. After the introduction, an historical account of the area is provided. "Location" describes how to find the campground, and "Facilities" describes the services offered at the park. Under the subheading of "Recreational

A camper's home is his castle—at any age.

Activities," I include hiking, cycling, fishing, boating, wildlife viewing, and family activities. "Rainy-day activities" include things to do near the campground. The "Summary" subsection provides personal and anecdotal information.

MAP OF BRITISH COLUMBIA CAMPGROUNDS

A — Porpoise Bay Provincial Park
B — Alice Lake Provincial Park
c — Sasquatch Provincial Park
D — Manning Provincial Park
E — Gordon Bay Provincial Park
F — Rathtrevor Beach
  Provincial Park
G — Montague Harbour
  Provincial Marine Park

H — Shuswap Lake Provincial Park
I — Ellison Provincial Park
J — Bear Creek Provincial Park
K — Okanagan Lake Provincial Park
L — Haynes Point Provincial Park
M — Kikomun Creek
  Provincial Park
N — Kokanee Creek Provincial Park
O — Kootenay National Park

MAP OF ALBERTA CAMPGROUNDS

A — Waterton Lakes National Park

B — Peter Lougheed Provincial Park

C — William A. Switzer Provincial Park

D — Aspen Beach Provincial Park

E — Bow Valley Provincial Park

F — Writing-on-Stone/Aisinai'pi Provincial Park

G — Cypress Hills Inter-Provincial Park

H — Dinosaur Provincial Park

I — Kinbrook Island Provincial Park

J — Whitney Lakes Provincial Park

PART I

BC—Lower Mainland, Vancouver Island, and Gulf Islands

→ Porpoise Bay Provincial Park

My prevailing image of Porpoise Bay is of family-friendly facilities; excellent services; large, private, well-maintained wooded camping spaces; beautiful scenery, including a sandy beach; and a nearby town—perfect for a family vacation. Porpoise Bay is unique as it has a no-fire policy, meaning all firepits have been removed, thereby giving the camping spots a slightly unfurnished appearance. A notice

The wide sandy beach at Porpoise Bay is perfect for young children.

on the park's information board explains the decision: "BC Parks has responded to requests by the community and some campers to improve the air quality by reducing the number of firepits in the park. At the same time, it is recognized campfires are a special part of the camping experience." Consequently, three communal firepits remain, so you can still roast a hot dog or toast a marshmallow and enjoy the experience of the campfire with other campers. I camped here every year when my kids were under five, which is in itself a testimonial to just how good this place is for young children.

History

The original inhabitants of the area were the Shíshálh (Sechelt) people, who hunted and fished in the region between the Strait of Georgia and Porpoise Bay. In the eighteenth century, British and Spanish explorers roamed the coastline. In 1986, the local Sechelt band became the first in Canada to be given authority to manage their land.

Location

Porpoise Bay Provincial Park is on the Sunshine Coast, which stretches along the northeastern side of the Strait of Georgia between Howe Sound to the south and Desolation Sound to the north. To reach this campground, you take an excursion on BC Ferries from Horseshoe Bay, where an excellent kids' playground can be found beside the ferry terminal—should you arrive with time to kill. Catch the ferry from Horseshoe Bay to Langdale, a forty-five-minute sailing, and then follow Highway 101 to the centre of Sechelt (25 kilometres), where the paved, 5-kilometre Porpoise Bay Road leads to the campground. The 61-hectare park is located on the east side of the Sechelt Inlet.

Facilities

Campers here want for nothing as Porpoise Bay has flush and pit toilets, showers, a sani-station, wheelchair access, and it also accepts reservations.

There are eighty-four large gravel camping spots, including a few double units in a second-growth forest of Douglas fir, western red cedar, western hemlock, and alder. As mentioned above, fires are prohibited in individual campsites, but are permitted in the three communal pits between 5:00 p.m. and 10:30 p.m. The campground has an area specifically designed for camping cyclists, which can accommodate up to forty people. All services are found 5 kilometres away in Sechelt, including a McDonald's and a growing number of very good bakeries, coffee shops, and restaurants.

Recreational Activities

HIKING A number of trails ribbon throughout the park. The most popular is the Angus Creek Trail, which leads to a tree-lined stream that is a spawning waterway for chum and coho salmon in the fall. Interpretative boards describe this process. Another trail leads to the marsh area of the inlet. At low tide, it is great to take the kids and just wander along the shoreline. Lifting stones reveals scampering crabs, and the rock pools offer small fish, shrimp, and jellyfish—great for the collection bucket (but remember to put them back).

CYCLING The quiet roads adjacent to the campground and a number of mountain bike specific trails in the vicinity means the campground is great for those with a passion for cycling.

FISHING When we last visited, we saw numerous fish jumping out of the water only a stone's throw from the swimming area. Fishing in the inlet and the various rivers and streams can yield coho salmon and cod. There are also fantastic opportunities for young kids to catch toe-biters with nets in the shallow water of the protected swimming area.

BOATING The park functions as a base for kayakers, who use it to explore the many coves and inlets of the surrounding area. Porpoise Bay is near the Sechelt Inlet Provincial Marine Recreational Area, which includes eight wilderness campsites located on the sheltered water of the Sechelt Inlet—a paddler's dream. The area is also rich in marine life. Therefore, although Porpoise Bay is especially popular with families, those who like to paddle can also find tranquillity here amid the West Coast scenery.

WILDLIFE VIEWING Porpoise Bay is widely recommended as a wildlife viewing location. You are likely to see loons, grebes, cormorants, ducks, and bald eagles, especially if you are walking around the campground first thing in the morning with young children. Information boards detail when each type of bird visits the park and your chances of seeing them.

FAMILY ACTIVITIES One of the biggest attractions here is the wide, sandy beach and the protected shallow swimming area, ideal for young children. A grassy field with picnic tables, toilets, playground, and change house is adjacent to the beach, and at suppertime this area is crowded with parents trying to exhaust their kids before bed. It's a lovely meeting place. There is a great field for all games in the centre of the campground, and a number of sites have direct access to it. When we camped here on one occasion, our kids ran around this space and were taught boules (a French form of lawn bowling) by another group of older children while we cooked dinner. Float planes take off and land at the other side of the inlet, providing an interesting although somewhat noisy distraction.

RAINY-DAY ACTIVITIES The nearby bustling community of Sechelt is a pleasant place to explore. One of the most impressive buildings in the town is the House of Hewhiwus (House of Chiefs), a massive cultural centre containing the offices of the Sechelt Indian Government District as well as a museum, theatre, and gift shop. The staff members at the Sechelt visitor centre can give you advice on hiking, kayaking, fishing, diving, cycling, and golf in the area. You can take a lovely quiet drive up the Sunshine Coast north of Sechelt. Skookumchuck Narrows Provincial Park, at the north end of the Sechelt Peninsula, is well worth a visit, especially if you plan your arrival to coincide with the peak tidal flows. Alternatively, travel 25 kilometres south to the community of Gibsons, famous for the *Beachcombers* TV series and a quaint maritime museum.

Summary

Porpoise Bay is an excellent family campground, close to all amenities. Many have recognized its advantages, so you should make reservations if you plan to camp in July or August.

Finally, I have to add that this is one of the quietest campgrounds I know. Even when it is full, everyone seems to be in bed by 10:00 p.m. I attribute this to the lack of campfires, which means that few noisy alcohol-induced conversations occur, as there are no glowing embers to congregate around. In sharp contrast to many other campgrounds in the Lower Mainland, Porpoise Bay is really quiet. And for this reason, and a multitude of others, it should be on every camper's list of must-visit spots. It is the perfect place for the family with young children.

→ Alice Lake Provincial Park

Alice Lake is not far from Vancouver, but still provides that get-away-from-it-all experience.

Alice Lake is my favourite campground to escape to quickly. We can leave our home in Vancouver and be there in ninety minutes. In June and September, as long as it's not a hot weekend, we can easily find space, although chances of finding space in July and August are slim to non-existent. A Tim Hortons restaurant is only a twelve-minute drive from the campground (this fact has been very well researched), should one decide to indulge in sandwiches and doughnuts under the stars. And yet, despite this urban access, Alice Lake still provides that get-away-from-it-all experience. This was the park in which all four of us first camped together under canvas, so I am sentimentally attached to it. We all went to bed at 7:30 p.m., giggled, and told stories in the tent until it got dark (8:30 p.m.—it was September), whereupon the kids went to sleep and we lay awake watching them in the half light, eventually being lulled to sleep by their breathing. Camping does create wonderful memories.

History

Alice Lake is close to the community of Brackendale, once larger than Squamish but now part of that municipality. Squamish, meaning "Mother of the Wind," has been settled since the late nineteenth century, when pioneers from Europe arrived to log giant cedar and fir trees, which were then tied together and floated across Howe Sound to the population centres farther south. Alice Lake was named after Alice Rose who, with her husband Charlie, was among the first settlers in the region. They built a homestead in the 1880s and earned a living by logging and farming. The provincial park was established in 1956.

Location

The park is easily accessible from Vancouver on Highway 99—the Sea to Sky Highway—13 kilometres north of Squamish. Nearby Brackendale is home to the largest population of bald eagles in North America. Visitors to Alice Lake have a good chance of seeing these splendid birds, but they are not the only attraction in this extremely popular park. There are also four lakes: Alice (the largest, covering 11.5 hectares), Stump, Fawn, and Edith.

Facilities

The 108 large, private, shady camping spots are suitable for all camping vehicles (55 have power hook-ups) and are situated in a forest of western hemlock. There are also 12 walk-in sites. Paved roads ribbon throughout the campground, which is equipped with showers, flush and pit toilets, and a sani-station. Alice Lake offers disabled access and accepts reservations. A small store selling coffee, ice cream, candy, chips, and beach toys operates in July and August in the day-use area. There are a couple of small stores in Brackendale, and Squamish has all services. Additional supplies can be found along the highway between Squamish and the park (e.g., A&W, Tim Hortons, Canadian Tire, and Starbucks).

Recreational Activities

HIKING For the ambitious, Alice Lake is a base from which to explore Garibaldi Provincial Park. Garibaldi covers almost 200,000 hectares, and during the summer months, you can hike to alpine meadows, glaciers, and mountains. Much of Garibaldi and the surrounding area is forested with fir, hemlock, red cedar, and balsam. In summer, it displays a breathtaking blanket of alpine flowers, making hikes in the area well worth the effort. For the less adventurous, there are a series of walking trails at Alice Lake itself. One of the most popular is the Four Lakes Trail, an easy, 6-kilometre (2-hour) walk with minimal elevation gain that takes hikers around the four warm-water lakes dominating the area; it's varied and kids can easily complete it. Interpretative boards posted on the section around Stump Lake describe the area's natural history. Numerous physical reminders of past logging operations are clearly visible from the trail. Another trail leads up Debecks Hill. From here you can enjoy views of the area that was shaped by volcanic activity thousands of years ago.

CYCLING A number of gravel roads attractive to mountain bikers run throughout the park. Some of the trails are closed to cyclists during the summer months, but are open at other times. The paved roads in the park are great for kids cycling and rollerblading, as are the quiet roads adjacent to the campground. This park is also ideal for the teenagers to go off and explore by themselves.

FISHING At the southern end of Alice Lake there is a pier, popular with fishers, from which you can cast your line for cutthroat, rainbow trout, and Dolly Varden. In May one year, we watched a father and his seven-year-old son catch nine trout from the children's swimming area in the space of forty minutes. Quite a stunning sight, for, as most would agree, you never usually see fishermen catch anything. The three other lakes also offer fishing possibilities: Edith, Stump, and Fawn lakes are stocked annually with rainbow trout.

BOATING All four lakes have paddling potential, with Alice Lake being the most popular site. Motorized crafts are prohibited on all lakes, which makes canoeing, kayaking, and fishing tranquil pursuits. Canoes can be rented in the park in July and August.

FAMILY ACTIVITIES Because Alice Lake is close to Vancouver, it attracts a great number of Lower Mainland families during the summer months—and for good reason. It has wonderful beaches for sunbathing or playing, clear weed-free water for swimming, a large grassy area for ball games next to the kids' beach, numerous picnic tables, and a change house. Swimming areas are cordoned off from the open lake, and there are wooden rafts to swim to. The beach, with its great sand for sandcastle building, is the main attraction, as is the view of the snow-capped mountains that encircle the lake. The water in the lake can be cold, but when did that ever bother the under-five age group? There is an adventure playground nicely positioned in the shade, and as this campground does attract so many families, it's the sort of place where your kids will make friends very easily.

RAINY-DAY ACTIVITIES In recent years, the community of Squamish has grown and now boasts several attractions, including a railway museum with a number of trains from a bygone age, some faithfully restored and others waiting to be returned to their former glory. One of the highlights of visiting this museum is the chance to speak to the volunteers and staff, who tell interesting stories about the trains' histories. There is also a really neat miniature railway to ride. It's easy to spend two to three hours here and is well worth a visit even if you're not camping. Squamish also has a golf course, a museum, and a number of commercial facilities that offer such things as helicopter tours of the nearby glaciers or whitewater rafting excursions. The Sea to Sky Gondola is another stellar attraction nearby, taking passengers from Shannon Falls Provincial Park to the top of the Stawamus Chief, 885 metres above sea level.

The Tenderfoot Fish Hatchery is located just outside Brackendale and has exhibits of chinook, coho, and steelhead (free admission), and is a nice bike ride for older kids. South of Squamish is the BC Museum of

Wading in the weed-free waters of Alice Lake.

Mining, which is ideal for kids over the age of seven. Here you don hard hats and take a train ride underground for a really informative tour. North of the campground is Brandywine Falls Provincial Park, where a short walk leads to some spectacular falls. Finally, of course, if the weather is really bad, think of visiting Whistler, only an hour's drive farther north, for a bit of window shopping and strolling. Here the Starbucks and Blenz coffee bars are located directly in front of the children's play area, so you can enjoy a cappuccino and watch the kids have fun too.

Summary

Alice Lake is a very popular location, even during the week, and is frequently full over the peak summer months. It is ideal if your children are two, twelve, or twenty-two. In June, it is already too late to reserve a camping spot for a weekend in July and August, so if you arrive during these times without a reservation, make sure you have a backup plan. One option is Nairn Falls Provincial Park, north of Whistler. It is not as popular as Alice Lake, but has camping facilities as well, and as long as you arrive before 5:00 p.m., there is a better chance of finding a spot.

→ Sasquatch Provincial Park

Swimming is delightful in Sasquatch Lake Provincial Park.

A ny first-time visitor to this provincial park cannot help but be in awe of the area's stunning scenery. As you travel the final stretch from Harrison Hot Springs to the gates of the campground, the paved road twists and turns along the edge of Harrison Lake and offers a stunning vista. When we last camped here, it was warm when we arrived at Lakeside Campground and we all managed a swim in Deer Lake. We had the lake to ourselves, as we were the only ones in the water. Floating on your back, staring up at the blue sky in the middle of the lake surrounded by high, forested mountains is truly magical. Upon arrival, make sure you and the kids keep an eye out for the mythical Sasquatch, also known as Bigfoot, which is reputed to prowl around the mountains and valleys of the area.

Alice Lake has a lakeside beach that is perfect for kids.

Fishing at Deer Lake and playing at Harrison Lake—two of the four lakes in Sasquatch Provincial Park.

Ellison Provincial Park in the Okanagan. TREVOR JULIER (ABOVE)

Bear Creek is one of the most popular provincial parks in the Okanagan. TREVOR JULIER

A clean, sandy beach at Kokanee Creek Provincial Park. TREVOR JULIER

The SS Moyie, the last sternwheeler to service Kootenay Lake, is now a great museum.
TREVOR JULIER

Fort Steele's fully restored heritage structures are well worth a visit. TREVOR JULIER

The Kootenay ferry, which travels across Kootenay Lake from Balfour to Kootenay Bay, was once the longest free ferry ride in the world. Kids love the thirty-five-minute trip, and parents will love the price! TREVOR JULIER

The Kettle Valley Railway in Summerland operates a quaint steam train over the summer months. TREVOR JULIER

Radium Hot Springs are BC's best-known hot springs, with over 400,000 visitors per year.
TREVOR JULIER

The water park on Kelowna's waterfront is always a treat for kids.

The warm waters of Okanagan Lake are heavenly.

No BC camping trip would be complete without wildlife spotting. TREVOR JULIER

Seeing animals in the wild is a great opportunity to teach kids about nature. TREVOR JULIER

You may have to share your spot on the waterfront with these curious critters. TREVOR JULIER

Always use caution when camping in bear country. TREVOR JULIER

History

The name "Sasquatch" is an English corruption of the Coast Salish word *Sasqac*. The *Sasqac* is a mythical creature, half man and half beast, which should be avoided. Local Aboriginal bands still report sightings of the Sasquatch around Harrison River, so be warned!

The area is famous for its hot springs, and Harrison Hot Springs calls itself "the Spa of Canada." The Coast Salish people first revered the therapeutic waters as a healing place. Europeans discovered them in 1859 when a pioneer fell out of his canoe into Harrison Lake, and instead of perishing in cold water, found the lake to be warm. Development started in 1885 when a hotel and bathhouse were built. The water rights to the hot mineral waters are still held by the Harrison Hot Springs Hotel.

Harrison Lake is over 60 kilometres long, making it the largest body of fresh water in southwestern BC; the glaciers of the Coast Mountains, north of Pemberton, melt into it. In the 1850s, it was on the gold rush route for prospectors travelling between the Fraser River and the goldfields in the Cariboo. At the end of the nineteenth century, logging started around the lake and is still the main local industry. Huge logging trucks are a regular feature on the roads. Today, Harrison Hot Springs attracts thousands of tourists throughout the year, but somehow manages to retain a quaint village atmosphere.

Location

It is easy to see why this park is such a popular family location: it contains four pristine lakes, including the freshwater fjord of massive Harrison Lake, and over 1,220 hectares of land. It is a vast expanse to explore in the midst of beautiful mountain scenery. Sasquatch Provincial Park is located 6 kilometres north of Harrison Hot Springs. Take Highway 9 from the junction of Highway 7 to Harrison Hot Springs (6.5 kilometres), and then take Rockwell Drive to the park entrance. A good gravel road leads into the park and to the campgrounds, 5 kilometres from the park gate. Watch out for logging trucks.

Facilities

In many respects, Sasquatch is not one provincial park but three, as there are three campgrounds here, all quite separate from each other, offering a total of 177 spaces. Of the three, Hicks Lake Campground would be my third choice, as the camping spots are smaller than the ones found in most BC parks, and some are very close together and confined (spaces 18, 19, and 20, for example, are more like parking spaces than camping spots). Bench Campground is near Deer Lake, although it does not have direct access to the lake. The spots are well situated in a forested area, and there are a number of double spots. Be advised there is little chance of the sun breaking through, as these sites are heavily shaded by trees. My favourite campground at Sasquatch is Lakeside, where a number of spots have direct access onto the lake (try 28, 31, or 32). Even if you are not fortunate enough to obtain one of these perfect sites, all the others at this location are large and in a forested area—great for kids.

All three campgrounds have pit toilets, water pumps, and there is a sani-station but no showers. The campgrounds are not wheelchair accessible. The park accepts reservations and is very popular in the peak summer months. Services available in Harrison Hot Springs include a number of restaurants, pizza parlours, ice cream stores, coffee bars (the one at the Harrison Hot Springs Hotel opens around 6:30 a.m.—ideal if that's the time your baby is awake), shops, and boutiques.

Recreational Activities

HIKING There are two trails located near Hicks Lake. One is a 4-kilometre hike around the lake. This trail may be muddy if the weather has been wet, but otherwise it is an ideal family hike. The other, Beaver Lodge Trail, is an easy twenty-minute stroll around a small lake with a beaver lodge. Interpretative boards have been placed along the trail to explain the beavers' habitat and the fish-spawning process. Lakeside Trail at Deer Lake is an easy, short walk to a lookout where you might see mountain goats on the nearby bluffs.

CYCLING The gravel roads that lead to the three camping locations are ideal for mountain biking, and the roads and trails in all campgrounds are safe for children to cycle around.

FISHING Trout fishing is reputed to be excellent at this park, and you might also catch kokanee in the lakes. In addition to lake fishing, you can try your luck in the waters of the Harrison and Fraser Rivers. Little toe-biters can easily be caught with nets in Deer Lake.

BOATING The four lakes at this location (Harrison, Hicks, Deer, and Trout) vary in size and in the recreational pursuits they offer. Harrison and Hicks permit powerboats, while only electric motors are allowed at Deer Lake. Powerboats are also prohibited at Trout Lake, and consequently, it is ideal for canoeing and kayaking. Boaters should be careful of deadheads, and of the winds that often come up on the larger lakes. Canoe rentals are available at Hicks and Deer Lakes.

FAMILY ACTIVITIES With four lakes to choose from, swimming here is delightful. Two beach locations at Hicks Lake ensure sun-worshipping

Sasquatch is a real gem for fishing and boating.

opportunities; one is at the southern end, and one is by the group camping area. From this second location, it is possible to swim to two small, forested islands that are ideal for exploring. There is a small beach and large grassy area leading to Deer Lake, and also a jetty to sunbathe on. Be warned that the grass near the swimming beaches can be well speckled with the evidence of Canada geese. The day-use area in the park on Harrison Lake has a wonderful beach, a grassy picnic area, and changing facilities, but the water of the lake is considerably colder than that of Deer Lake. More adventurous campers can windsurf, water ski, or jet ski. The lagoon pool in the town of Harrison Hot Springs has a sandy beach and playground on the beach, which my kids really liked. A play area for children is located at the Lakeside Campground. The town is famous for its mineral pools and for its annual sand sculpture contest in September (see next topic).

RAINY-DAY ACTIVITIES The picturesque community of Harrison Hot Springs is a lovely place to wander about. There is a beach, and you can arrange excursions on the lake through the summer months. A lakeside trail starting from Harrison Hot Springs Hotel takes you to a structure housing the emerging hot springs; you can put your hand in and feel the warm water. The building is dilapidated so do not expect a photo opportunity. To truly experience the therapeutic waters, you must book into the Harrison Hot Springs Hotel, or visit the local swimming pool (the cheaper alternative). The pool is also a good place to take a hot shower if you and your offspring have not felt warm water for a few days. The public pool rents lockers, towels, and swimsuits, and is open seven days a week. I advise anyone who has not experienced hot pools to try them, but don't expect to want to do much afterwards other than sleep; they have a very soporific effect.

Each year, Harrison Hot Springs holds a sand sculpture competition, with entrants from all over the world. Sand sculptures in the shape of Elvis, castles, loggers, mythical creatures, and more are on show from mid-September until mid-October. In July, Harrison Hot Springs has an annual festival of the arts, which includes craft sales and free concerts.

Summary

Sasquatch is a super place for family camping and is a provincial park where, if the weather is good, it is easy to spend a week's vacation. Although there are not a lot of hiking trails, if your family enjoys swimming, sunbathing, fishing, boating, or just having fun surrounded by amazing scenery, then Sasquatch is a real gem. Its easy access to the town of Harrison Hot Springs means campers should not be at a loss for things to do, even if the weather is bad, and there are a lot of places to choose from for eating out. Though it may be cold in the tent, the knowledge that hot mineral pools are only a twenty-minute drive away will keep all visitors, whatever their age, happy and relaxed campers. In addition, because Sasquatch is a little farther away from the Lower Mainland than Alice Lake or Golden Ears, it is not so popular and therefore more likely to have an available space. If the weather report on Wednesday says there's going to be good weather over the weekend, you'll probably be able to reserve a space—even in July and August.

→ Manning Provincial Park

Having fun with Dad in the playground at Manning Park.

Unlike many provincial parks, which open in April with a season extending until October, summer activities in Manning are confined to the period between the end of May and September. I once stayed here during the Victoria Day weekend in late May, when cross-country skiing and snowshoeing were the most popular activities and only one trail was open for hiking. If you are planning a trip to this park early in the season, you may want to telephone the visitor centre to determine which facilities are open. While the sun could be shining in Vancouver, the snow may not have thawed here. Having said that, it is a huge park with so many activities and services that even if you have to abandon the tent for a room at the lodge, you and the kids are bound to have fun and find plenty to do.

History

Manning Park is named after E.C. Manning, chief forester of British Columbia from 1936 to 1941. It developed from the Three Brothers Mountain Reserve, created in 1931 to save the alpine meadows from overgrazing by mountain sheep. When the Hope–Princeton Highway opened to the public in 1945, Manning became a popular vacation spot with residents of the Lower Mainland and remains so today. It frequently ranks as the third most popular campground in the province (after Golden Ears and Rathtrevor). Its history dates back to the First Nations people, who visited the area to hunt and fish; the present Skyline Trail was a well-used route for these early residents.

Location

The park covers over 65,000 hectares within the Cascade Mountains and encompasses two major river systems: the Skagit, which flows to the Pacific Ocean, and the Similkameen, which joins the Okanagan River to the east. The main park administrative centre is between Hope and Princeton. The park itself is within a three-hour drive from Vancouver (224 kilometres) and is located on Highway 3, 30 kilometres east of Hope. If you are travelling to Manning by car from Vancouver, take the more northerly Route 7 instead of Route 1, as it is a far more scenic drive. Kilby is an ideal spot to break the journey because it's about midway between Vancouver and Manning, and it includes a small farm, café, shop, and restored general store dating back to the 1920s. The Kilby General Store Museum features not only a cornucopia of long-forgotten items on all of the shelves, but also a downstairs store where children can use period weight scales, a crank telephone, and an apple press.

Facilities

There are four main campgrounds in Manning Park with a total of 355 camping spaces: Hampton (99); Mule Deer (49); Coldspring (64); and

Lightning Lake (143). All spaces at Lightning Lake are reservable, which means campers arriving without reservations are restricted to the other three campgrounds if Lightning Lake is full. Lightning Lake is the only campground with showers and flush toilets and is close to the beach, so it is the preferred camping location if you have young ones to entertain, or if you require the luxury of showers. A sani-station is located near the visitor centre. All the camping spots in the four campgrounds are large and private, and in a well-forested environment. Some sites at Coldspring and Mule Deer are near the river. Unfortunately, traffic noise is audible at Mule Deer, Coldspring, and Hampton, but the traffic isn't heavy during the evening or night.

Manning Park Lodge provides lodge rooms, cabins, chalets, a licensed restaurant, a pub, a coffee bar, and a shop that sells a range of provisions for camping. It rents mountain bikes, canoes, kayaks, rowboats, snowshoes, and skis. The lodge also offers tennis courts, swimming pool, hot tub, dry and wet saunas, and an exercise room; kids under seventeen stay free if sharing a room with an adult.

Recreational Activities

HIKING The first port of call for anyone visiting Manning should be the visitor centre, a kilometre east of Manning Park Lodge, to collect a detailed map of the area and to see the displays of stuffed animals and birds. Manning is a true hiker's paradise with over 276 kilometres of trails. There are self-guided nature trails, short easy walks ideal for younger kids (Engineers Loop, Rain Orchid, Twenty Minute Lake, Strawberry Flats, Dry Ridge, Viewpoint Trail), and much longer hikes. One of the most popular longer hikes is the Skyline Trail, which follows the north ridge to Lightning Lake with an elevation gain of 460 metres. For those who like a long walk without the uphill climb, Lightning Lake Chain Trail is an easy 24-kilometre hike along the sides of four lakes. When I once did this walk, hiking with an eight-month-old on my back, I saw deer, beaver, and grouse. Hiking the 21-kilometre Heather Trail in July and August is well worth the effort, as more than a hundred species of wild alpine flowers bloom in what BC Parks describes as "a floral carpet more than 24 kilometres in length and up to 5 kilometres in width." One advantage of this trail is that because you drive to the top of a mountain to access it, you have ample energy to marvel at the views. I adore this walk and cannot recommend it too highly. The photographic opportunities are second to none.

CYCLING You can rent mountain bikes from the boathouse at Lightning Lake. Mountain bikes are permitted on the 14-kilometre Windy Joe Trail and the 32-kilometre Monument 83 Trail.

FISHING Anglers can fish for Dolly Varden or rainbow and cutthroat trout in the Similkameen and Sumallo rivers, while fly casters can try for rainbow trout in Lightning and Strike lakes. Fishing licences are available at the front desk of Manning Park Lodge and tackle can be purchased from the resort store.

BOATING Powerboats are prohibited in the park. Canoeing is a joy at Lightning Lake, where there is a launch for car-top boats in the day-use area. As mentioned above, kayaks, canoes, and rowboats can be rented from the Lodge shop and, during the peak months of July and August, from the Lightning Lake day-use area.

WILDLIFE OBSERVATION A wide variety of wildlife lives within the park, including over 190 different species of birds, which makes the area popular with ornithologists. It is not unusual to see black bears at the side of the road in the springtime. Although a number of people are somewhat uneasy about sharing Manning Park with the resident bears, it should be noted that there has never been a bear attack in over fifty years of the park's existence.

FAMILY ACTIVITIES Displays of the area's human and natural history are in the visitor centre, along with an abundance of other information. There is a small play area for children next to Manning Park

Lodge with a huge bear sculpture. This is also the place to chase hordes of ground squirrels back into their holes—an activity sure to exhaust all involved except the creatures themselves. Lightning Lake has a beach and safe swimming area, hence the benefit of staying at this campground and not the others. Indeed, many families seem to never leave this location.

RAINY-DAY ACTIVITIES The two towns on either side of Manning Park both have something to offer the visitor. Hope promotes itself as the "Chainsaw Carving Capital of the World," and has a rapidly expanding number of chainsaw statues. It has a small museum and is a pleasant river town with all amenities and a good playground in the centre of town. When you travel from Manning to Hope, be sure to stop at the Hope Slide. A plaque and viewpoint indicate the area where, in January 1965, a side of Johnson Peak plunged into the valley, covering the highway with 45 metres of rubble. Also near Hope and not to be missed are the Kettle Valley Railway tunnels. This is an impressive series of five large tunnels that were cut through the granite walls of the Coquihalla Canyon. Named after Shakespearean characters, they last saw railway traffic in 1959; in 1986, they were opened by the provincial parks ministry as the Coquihalla Canyon Recreational Area. Visitors now walk through these tunnels to the sound of roaring water below. The tunnels are signposted from the Coquihalla Highway and are well worth a visit. Remember to bring a flashlight and a camera.

Summary

Because Manning is such a large park, it never feels crowded in spite of its high level of use. It's a great place to holiday with your family because you can hike one day, canoe the next, sunbathe the next, and, if you still have energy, ride a mountain bike, swim, and chase ground squirrels. We have camped here when the kids were small, and then as they reached their teens, we took them on a hiking/camping vacation, proving that Manning is suitable for every age. I also particularly appreciate the facilities it offers. On those cold, wet mornings when you wake up and can't face the task of trying to make a fire with wood sodden by last night's rain, it is a real comfort to know that hot coffee and a cooked breakfast can be had, at a reasonable price, only a few kilometres away at the lodge. The washroom facilities also add a level of comfort, of course. While this may not accord with the true camping spirit, even a seasoned camper can appreciate some luxury from time to time.

Dad hikes with eight-month-old Jack.

→ Gordon Bay Provincial Park

The main attraction at Gordon Bay is swimming in the clear waters of Cowichan Lake.

McDonald, French Beach, Bamberton, Goldstream, and Gordon Bay are all beautiful campgrounds not too far from the main population centres of southern Vancouver Island and are relatively close to each other, which makes picking one over another a difficult decision. Gordon Bay is probably the best family campground, as it offers something for every age group, has excellent facilities, is only a short distance from a picturesque community, and yet is remote enough to have that get-away-from-it-all feel. There can be no better place for sun lovers as Gordon Bay Provincial Park's 49 hectares are located in one of the warmest valleys on Vancouver Island. The mountains pressing close around Cowichan Lake produce a heat trap that often ensures the campground has some of the highest average daily temperatures in Canada. The water of Cowichan Lake offers relief from this heat, as do the shady camping spots.

History

The area has a rich logging history, evident on the mountain slopes surrounding the valley. Logging, still a major industry here today, started in the 1880s, when oxen were used to haul felled wood. The area was also mined for copper, and the remains of the copper mine can be seen from the well-maintained logging road that rings the lake. When driving to the campground, there are a number of huge logging trucks on the road. The community of Honeymoon Bay, adjacent to the campground, is named after two early settlers, Henry and Edith March, who spent their honeymoon here. Prior to the immigration of European settlers, Coast Salish people lived here, hunting and fishing in the region.

Location

Gordon Bay Provincial Park is on the southern shore of Cowichan Lake, 35 kilometres west of Duncan, 14 kilometres west of the town of Lake Cowichan, and 2 kilometres from the small community of Honeymoon Bay. You can get to it by taking Highway 18, just north of Duncan, about a thirty-five-minute drive on a really good road.

Facilities

Situated in an area of second-growth Douglas fir, this campground has 122 large, nicely laid-out camping spots. There are flush and pit toilets, a sani-station, two shower buildings, and full disabled access. All spots are gravel, large enough to accommodate every type of recreational vehicle, and there are a number of double spots. Reservations are accepted and advisable, as this campground can get very full.

The nearby community of Lake Cowichan has restaurants, accommodation, food stores, gas station, a pub, and most amenities. Honeymoon Bay, just a couple of kilometres from the campground, has a good general store that sells camping supplies, candy, pop, and ice cream.

Recreational Activities

HIKING A number of trails lead through the park over a forest floor covered with thimbleberry, salal, salmonberry, and, in the spring, wonderful wildflowers. (Remember, picking vegetation in BC parks is prohibited.) The Point Trail leads from the beach to an area of rock overlooking the lake. You can swim here, away from the crowds. Interpretative signs along the route explain the plant life in the area. It takes about thirty minutes to complete this hike. Another trail, which takes two hours to complete, leads from the parking area, through some yellow gates, and past a small lake onto the logging road that rims the lake. You wind up at a viewpoint from which the full beauty of Cowichan Lake can be appreciated.

CYCLING The paved roads of the campground allow pleasant, safe cycling excursions for the young. Numerous logging roads nearby make mountain biking a good alternative for older kids. Also, it is an easy bicycle ride on a quiet road from the campground to the ice cream store at Honeymoon Bay, an ideal early-evening activity. Older kids should enjoy cycling on the quiet road to Lake Cowichan.

Bicycles rest while campers enjoy the playground.

Bikes are a great way to get around in Gordon Bay Provincial Park.

FISHING The fishing here is reputed to be excellent, as the lake has Dolly Varden, rainbow and cutthroat trout, chum, coho, and spring salmon for the angler. Fishing supplies are available in Honeymoon Bay. Sticklebacks and other small fry can be caught in nets from the beach.

BOATING There is a boat launch in the park, and waterskiing is permitted on the lake. Lake Cowichan, one of Vancouver Island's largest lakes, is 32 kilometres long and 3 kilometres wide, with plenty of room for powerboaters, jet skiers, canoists, kayakers, and windsurfers. Boats can be rented in Honeymoon Bay during the peak season.

FAMILY ACTIVITIES The biggest attraction here is undoubtedly the wonderful sandy/pebbly beach, and large swimming area devoid of weeds and sharp stones. It is difficult to find a more perfect lakeside beach, and although the water may feel cold at first, it provides a respite from the hot temperatures often experienced here. The swimming area is cordoned off by log booms, which children of every age love to balance on and dive from.

There are numerous picnic tables on a grassy area adjacent to the beach. Many are under the shade of the trees, but you will need to arrive early if you want to reserve one. An adventure playground has been constructed within the camping area, and interpretative programs take place during the summer. Just a short bike ride away in Honeymoon Bay, there is also a wonderful playground, which has all the usual climbing equipment as well as basketball hoops and hockey nets on a paved court. For those with older offspring, or access to babysitting for the young ones, there is an attractive nine-hole golf course at Honeymoon Bay, which also has a small restaurant overlooking the greens.

RAINY-DAY ACTIVITIES After you've enjoyed the beauty of the park, you can partake in the activities available in the surrounding area. A small museum at Saywell Park in the town of Lake Cowichan offers details about the local history. Those who want a broader picture can take a tour of the Lake Cowichan Earth Satellite Station. The Cowichan River meanders through the community, and it is possible to fish for trout in its water. An old wooden railway bridge is a novel way to cross the river.

The town of Duncan calls itself the "City of Totems" with more than eighty totem poles throughout the town; follow the painted footsteps for a tour. Duncan is also home to the world's largest hockey stick and a large leisure centre complete with hot tub and pool. Just north of Duncan, the smaller seaside community of Chemainus bills itself as the world's largest outdoor gallery, with over thirty-four murals and twelve sculptures. Chemainus is very kid friendly (if you avoid the craft and gift shops, which tend to be too full of breakable objects for my comfort), with two playgrounds, numerous ice cream stores and coffee bars, a large water wheel, and, in the summer, horse-drawn carriage rides. With all the murals to see in town, it's a great place to wander around.

Summary

Gordon Bay is a delightful, family-oriented camping location equipped with all amenities, but be warned: it is one of the most popular camp-grounds on southern Vancouver Island and is frequently full. I first stayed here mid-week in early June, when only half of the camping spots were open and the BC Parks workers were just gearing up for the peak season. At this time, my partner and I shared the beach with three other couples. We could see only two boats on the lake and were the only people brave enough to swim in the cold water. It was tranquil; it was beautiful; it was special. This experience was in sharp contrast to my second trip to enjoy the facilities of Gordon Bay, one weekday in August with my three- and four-year-olds. Five years after my initial visit, it was noisy; it was busy; it was stressful—but it was ideal for kids. In 2014, we visited again, in early June when it was very quiet with the only other campers being young parents with preschoolers— an under-five's paradise. Gordon Bay merits its reputation as one of the most popular family camping spots on Vancouver Island.

→ Rathtrevor Beach Provincial Park

Sea, sand, and plenty of driftwood attract campers to Rathtrevor Beach.

With over 160,000 visitors per year, this is Vancouver Island's most popular provincial park and one of the most popular in the province. Within the camping fraternity, stories circulate of the impossibility of finding a camping spot here in July and August, with lines of RVs waiting to get in. Anyone who has seen the 2,000 metres of beach and the first-rate camping facilities, including some of the largest, most private camping spots on the BC Parks roster, can easily understand its popularity. Rathtrevor is probably the perfect location—if the weather co-operates—for a family vacation.

History

Rathtrevor got its name from a gold prospector and pioneer, William Rath, who settled in the area with his wife and family in 1886. He died in 1903, leaving his wife with the farm and five children. To supplement her farming income, she started to charge visitors for picnicking on her land. Soon picnicking led to camping, and she charged a fee of twenty-five cents, then fifty cents per weekend (at press time, the camping fee was thirty-five dollars per night). Mrs. Rath eventually developed the land into a full campground and added the word "trevor" to the name for effect. BC Parks acquired Rathtrevor in 1967. The park started with 140 spots and four large parking areas and was expanded to 174 spaces in 1976. The visitor centre is located in the old family farmhouse.

Location

Rathtrevor Beach encompasses more than 347 hectares of land (including 2 kilometres of sandy shoreline) and is situated on Highway 19A, 2 kilometres south of Parksville (29 kilometres north of Nanaimo). It has views of the Strait of Georgia and the Coast Mountains on the mainland beyond. Interpretative boards located on the beach identify peaks in this mountain range, so you do not have to guess.

Facilities

It is not only the sea and sand that attract campers to this location. I believe the camping spots themselves are some of the best in the province. The 174 spacious sites are located in a forest of Douglas fir and accommodate every type of recreational vehicle. There are a number of double spots, and group camping is also available. The vegetation is quite dense, affording privacy from even the nearest neighbour. The campground is fully equipped with a sani-station, showers, flush and pit toilets (in 2014, a number of these toilets were brand new), and is wheelchair accessible throughout. The washrooms are tiled and have baby-changing facilities. A maze of paved roads with names such as Foam Flower Lane and Sea Blush Lane provides access to the sites. Reservations are accepted and advisable as the campground is *very* popular, especially during the months of July and August. Services are available in Parksville. A small concession at the visitor centre sells ice cream, pop, candy bars, chips, coffee, and toys, and at the entrance to the campground from the highway there is a log cabin store selling supplies.

Recreational Activities

HIKING There are over 4 kilometres of easy hiking trails in the park, leading through the wooded area and along the shore. There are also self-guided nature trails. Some trails are closed to cyclists. One of the best pastimes we found was beachcombing at low tide. There is also a trail, which runs parallel to the day-use area, and is a good place to people-watch.

CYCLING Children adore this location for cycling. The paved roads in the camping area and the many trails and quiet roads in the park are a safe cycling haven to explore. The paved roads are also a delight for rollerblading. In 2014, bike rental was a very affordable five dollars an hour.

BOATING You can windsurf and canoe here, but there is no boat launch.

WILDLIFE VIEWING Birdwatching is reputed to be good in the springtime and during the annual herring spawn.

FAMILY ACTIVITIES Famed for its beautiful sandy shingle leading to warm, clear water, Rathtrevor is "unbeatable for swimming," according to BC Parks literature. This is the perfect family beach campground for picnicking and playing in the safe water. Many families spend a week or longer just on the beach, which is well equipped with fresh water, a change house, and picnic tables. Dogs are prohibited on the beach. If you want to escape the crowds, you can find your own private beach spot on the waterfront closer to the campground, where there are more rocks and logs, but fewer people and less noise. Lots of washed-up logs in these more remote places are great places to build dens and play pirate games.

There are two children's play areas. In summer months, an amphitheatre is used to deliver visitor programs like "Freddy the Frog," "Critter Olympics," and "Bee Social." The visitor centre, open 11:00 a.m.

to 4:00 p.m. during the summer, has a first-class display of natural and human history artifacts, including a display of live bees, stuffed birds (including bald eagles, owls, and hawks), photographs showing the park's development and the logging history of the region, and marine life presentations. Staff members at this centre are keen to provide information about the animals and plants found in the park, in addition to offering advice on a multitude of other park-related issues.

RAINY-DAY ACTIVITIES There are a number of commercial facilities that have sprung up near the park. These include minigolf, go-karts, boat rentals, golf courses, water parks, and adventure playgrounds. The neighbouring community of Parksville is named after Nelson Park, one of the first settlers in the area, and has a street full of restaurants and fast-food outlets. It also boasts a small museum and one of the Island's oldest churches, St. Anne's Anglican Church, which was built in 1894.

Summary

This campground is extremely popular. However, if you arrive to find it full, you do not have far to travel to find alternative provincial

The visitor centre at Rathtrevor Beach Provincial Park is located in an old family farmhouse.

park camping. Englishman River Falls Provincial Park is only 13 kilometres away, and Little Qualicum Falls is 24 kilometres from Rathtrevor. Although Rathtrevor is extremely busy, the number of people employed to administer the park's facilities ensures that amenities are well cared for. While the camper relaxes on the beach, a platoon of workers empties the garbage, cleans bathrooms, rakes the gravel, and provides every type of help and assistance.

While the expense of taking the ferry may deter families off Vancouver Island, the size of the campground, the facilities offered, and the location make it one of the best campgrounds in BC—maybe even in Canada.

Rathtrevor's large camping spots are suitable for every size of camping vehicle.

→ Montague Harbour Provincial Marine Park

Still camping at eight months pregnant!

Two hours from downtown Vancouver or Victoria, a beautiful little campground waits with everything you need for a weekend escape from the city: calm sea waters, wide white beaches, shady camping spots, and a tranquillity that only an island can provide. I adore this place and camped here when I was eight months pregnant with my second son in August 2000. At this time, it was hot, but the shade of the camping spots and sea breeze made it bearable. I swaggered around the campground like a galleon in full sail with my baby bump leading the way, gaining sympathetic looks and comments from all the other campers. In my opinion, Galiano Island is the nicest of the Gulf Islands and a lovely, quiet place to camp.

History

The island is named after Dionisio Alcala Galiano, commander of the *Sutil*, who explored the area and claimed the island for Spain in 1792.

Shell middens at Montague Harbour, which are estimated to be over three thousand years old, testify to the much earlier, semi-permanent settlement of the Coast Salish people in the area. There is an archaeological site in the park where spearheads, carvings, and arrows have been found. One of the earliest European settlers on Galiano was a man named Henry Georgeson, who came from the Shetland Islands in the mid-1800s, purchased 59 hectares of land, and hunted deer. The people who settled on the island in the nineteenth century tended to build their homes at the south end of Galiano, near Whaler Bay, Sturdies Bay, and Georgeson Bay. Most of the island's thousand or so inhabitants still live in this area.

The twentieth century saw the development of a fishing industry. Herring was salted in five different places on Galiano; Japanese people ran four of the plants, while the fifth was a Chinese operation. A cannery and saltery were started on the island, but they were closed during the Second World War when the Japanese were interned and sent to the interior of BC. Today, many artists and craftspeople have chosen to live here, and there are a few restaurants, craft shops, and a first-rate bakery in the area around Sturdies Bay.

Location

Montague Harbour is BC's oldest marine park. When it opened in 1959, it was the first provincial park to serve visitors who arrived in boats as well as by car or on foot. The park encompasses an 89-hectare area that starts 5 metres below sea level and rises to 180 metres above. It includes a lagoon, a tidal salt marsh, a forest of various types of trees and undergrowth, a beach, cliffs, and rocks, and consequently is a varied and interesting place to explore or relax. If you do not have your own boat, you can reach Galiano Island via BC Ferries from Swartz Bay on Vancouver Island (about forty-five minutes) or from Tsawwassen on the mainland (about fifty minutes). Then drive 10 kilometres from Sturdies Bay to the park. During the summer months, ferry trips should be reserved (bcferries.com).

Facilities

There are forty well-positioned camping spots here; twenty-five are suitable for vehicles and are set in a forested area with Douglas fir, western hemlock, and western red cedar, while many of the fifteen walk-in sites overlook the harbour and have better views than the drive-in sites. The drive-in sites are large and accommodate almost all sizes of recreational vehicles. Group camping is also available, and there is an overflow site. Facilities are the basic ones found in BC Parks (pit toilets, water, picnic tables, firepits). There is no sani-station or disabled access. Reservations are accepted and advisable. There are a number of bed and breakfast accommodations, lodges, and cabins on the island. Most services are at Sturdies Bay, including a grocery and general store, restaurants, and a bakery that not only supplies tasty baked goods, but is also a great place to sit, drink coffee, and watch the world go by. You can rent kayaks and bicycles in the village (including bike trailers for kids). The marina adjacent to the campground has a small store and coffee bar where you can get some basic supplies. When we last stayed at Montague Harbour, this coffee bar served delicious freshly baked cinnamon buns first thing in the morning.

Recreational Activities

HIKING The longest trail takes you around Gray Peninsula, named after Captain Gray, an early explorer who settled on the island and cultivated an orchard that supplied fruit to the people of Victoria. This 3-kilometre trail follows the shoreline and lagoon around the peninsula, which was created by glacial action thousands of years ago. Other little trails zigzag their way around the campsites on the park's north side.

CYCLING While there is little opportunity for cycling in the campground itself, Galiano has lovely, quiet roads, especially once you leave the main population centre. Be warned, however, that Galiano is not by any means flat! Bikes can be rented in Sturdies Bay. Cyclists can easily travel the length of the island on Porlier Pass Road.

FISHING The area has abundant salmon and shellfish. This feature is not only appreciated by anglers, but also by the population of bald eagles and other birds that frequent the island.

BOATING There is a boat launch in the park, and kayaks can be rented from the nearby marina and at Sturdies Bay. Kayaking is a good way to explore the coastal scenery and is safe, as the waters of the bay are generally calm.

FAMILY ACTIVITIES This provincial park is suitable for retired individuals with time on their hands, and for families. The sandy, shell-covered beaches and the clear, warm water is perfect for swimming, beachcombing, and sunbathing, while the easy walks and trails within the park's boundaries are alternative attractions. There is a floating nature house in the park, and during the evening, you might find yourself looking through the transparent floor of this structure into the ocean to see the sea life. When we visited, the presenters gave fascinating accounts of the creatures that can be viewed in this magical way.

RAINY-DAY ACTIVITIES Montague Harbour is an ideal base from which to explore other Gulf Islands in your own craft or on BC Ferries. There are daily sailings to Mayne, Pender, Saturna, and Salt Spring Islands. If you have older children who like cycling, trips to the other Gulf Islands make great cycling excursions. Salt Spring is the largest Gulf Island, and in Ganges, the main centre, there is a good playground, numerous craft shops, and restaurants to explore, as well as a boardwalk around the harbour.

Summary

Galiano is smaller and less commercialized than Salt Spring Island, but offers more amenities than Pender. Montague Harbour is a park that can be appreciated by every age group. While I have attempted to describe the many activities available here, probably the best activity is to unwind and enjoy the beach. As the park is relatively small, the beach is never crowded, and you can spend many hours reading and building sandcastles by the calm water. In the evening, you can view breathtaking sunsets, and at night, the heavens explode with an abundance of stars that fill a sky far bigger than what you see in the city. If you need a change from campground food, try the Hummingbird Pub, which has a great outdoors area for kids to explore and excellent food, often accompanied by live entertainment. Be forewarned, though, as this establishment is very popular and has a great reputation, so it can get very busy. You may have to wait awhile for the culinary delights, but it will be worth it.

The boys bond on the beach.

PART 2

BC—The Okanagan
and the Rockies

→ Shuswap Lake Provincial Park

The boys enjoying a picnic with Dad at Shuswap Lake.

I f you are a camper who primarily enjoys hiking and exploring by land, and if you do not want to be surrounded by the younger generation, then you may decide that Shuswap is not the place to be, as this provincial park and its environs are family oriented, dominated by lake- and beach-based activities. However, if you are a camper who loves the water or has little ones to entertain, this is your paradise. Shuswap Lake, with over 1,000 kilometres of waterways that form an unconventional H shape, is a real magnet to the boating fraternity in the summer months. At the height of the season, 350 houseboats, together with many hundreds of smaller craft, sail the warm waters. But it is not only boaters who flock to its shores. Those with young children are drawn by the kilometre of fine beach and the hot climate that guarantees many days can be lazily spent enjoying the sun, water, and sand. And for those who just want to spend their time fishing, there is little to stop the pursuit of this pastime.

Shuswap Lake is actually made up of four arms: Shuswap Lake itself, Salmon Arm (connecting to Mara Lake), Anstey Arm, and Seymour Arm, which all meet at Cinnemousun Narrows. The only disadvantage to this water wonderland is that it does get extremely busy, with the main campground operating at capacity in July and August. Fortunately there are a number of campgrounds accessible only by boat, so for those with alternative modes of transport, peace is just a few knots away.

History

Shuswap Lake Provincial Park was created in 1956 and is the largest and most commercialized park in the Shuswap region, offering more than 270 spaces. The area is named after the Shuswap people (Secwepemc First Nation), the most northern of the Salishan language group, who were the first to appreciate this extensive inland water system and to enjoy the abundant natural resources. Evidence of these early inhabitants has been found in the form of kekulis—semi-underground pit houses built for enduring the winter—that have been found at Scotch Creek and at Herald Provincial Park. Pictographs or rock paintings are also visible on rock faces around the lake. Europeans arrived throughout the nineteenth century as fur traders, explorers, and then surveyors—working for the Canadian Pacific Railway—travelled the area. Gold was discovered in the region, which resulted in a flood of people. Towns and settlements rapidly appeared and disappeared as the gold prospectors arrived, worked the find, and moved on. Today little remains of their exploits.

Location

Shuswap Lake Provincial Park is on the lake from which it takes its name, on the old delta of Scotch Creek. The unusual lake formations are the result of glacial action that formed steep valley walls ringed by gently sloping mountainsides. The park is just under 150 hectares in area, and includes Copper Island, 2 kilometres offshore. Part of the reason for Shuswap's popularity is undoubtedly its central location, easily accessible from Highway 1. At Squilax, 90 kilometres east of Kamloops, turn off the highway onto a 20-kilometre twisting, paved road that leads to the campground. Most supplies can be found at a number of stores close to the entrance of the park, while more extensive supplies are available in Sorrento, 35 kilometres away.

Facilities

Because it is one of BC's largest provincial parks, the facilities offered at Shuswap Lake are comprehensive and include 274 camping spots suitable for every type of recreational vehicle, flush and pit toilets, sanistation, showers, and full disabled access. The camping spots are found in a dense second-growth forest of Douglas fir, aspen, white birch, and western red cedar. Reservations are accepted and strongly advised, as BC Parks says Shuswap Lake operates at full capacity from mid-July to Labour Day. This large provincial park is one of only three located on the lake that offers both vehicle and tent camping. The others are Herald (fifty-one spaces) and Silver Beach (thirty-five spaces). If you find Shuswap full, Silver Beach is the next closest to try. There are also wilderness campgrounds, only accessible by boat, at six locations on the lake.

Recreational Activities

HIKING Shuswap is not a great place for serious hiking. Next to the campground is a small nature trail, and there is a perimeter trail running near the park boundary, but neither takes more than an hour to complete. The perimeter trail had little to commend it, as I found myself walking by a large metal fence for a good portion of the way. There is a 3-kilometre trail on Copper Island that takes hikers to a viewpoint of the lake and area (remember the waterproof camera). During the summer, mule deer inhabit Copper Island. There are also short trails at Roderick Haig-Brown Provincial Park (see *Rainy-day activities*).

CYCLING One of the most popular recreational pursuits here is cycling, as there are over 11 kilometres of paved road in the park itself, and a mountain-bike trail has been developed. During the evening hours, the park is full of kids on rollerblades and bikes.

FISHING The entire Shuswap Lake system is known for good game-fish species, including rainbow trout, lake and brook trout, kokanee salmon, squawfish, burbot, carp, whitefish, and suckers. The best fishing months are May through June and October through November.

BOATING Water sports are popular here. There is a boat launch, and the waters attract powerboaters, water skiers, canoeists, kayakers, windsurfers, jet skiers, and houseboaters. As one would expect, the water is particularly busy near the campground and where the arms of the lake meet at Cinnemousun Narrows, but as there are four long arms to Shuswap Lake, it does not take too long to escape the crowd. You can rent canoes or kayaks at commercial outlets adjacent to the campground. Unfortunately the dreaded noisy jet ski can also be rented nearby. While there is no overnight boat mooring at Shuswap Lake, nearby Shuswap Lake Provincial Marine Park offers this facility as well as six separate developed and eight undeveloped camping locations along all four arms of the lake.

FAMILY ACTIVITIES This is a place for family fun, which centres on the kilometre-long beach. A safe swimming area with beautiful sand, warm water, and two diving platforms is the most popular area of the park from 9:00 a.m. until well into the evening hours. Shuswap Lake has a busy visitor centre, which provides historical information about the area. Shuswap boasts what must be one of the largest and most comprehensive children's play areas of any provincial park, and, as mentioned above, commercial Recreational Activities (for example, kayak rentals and go-karts) are easily accessible in the surrounding area.

RAINY-DAY ACTIVITIES Boaters do not have to be told about the massive expanse of lake and shoreline that is theirs to explore. For those who do not have access to this mode of transportation, Roderick Haig-Brown Provincial Park, less than 8 kilometres from Shuswap, is an alternative, especially if you plan to visit in September. This park on the Adams River is accessible to the spectacle of a major run of sockeye salmon. The fish return every year, but every four years the river turns red as approximately 1.5 million fish crowd into the area. During these peak years, BC Parks arranges a "Salute to the Salmon," with displays and additional staff on hand to describe the event. (The next spectacle occurs in 2018.) Even if your visit does not coincide with this event, it is worth visiting the park to learn of the salmon-spawning process and to walk the trails.

Summary

As mentioned above, this area is extremely popular during the summer months and may not be to everyone's taste at this time because it presents the more commercial side to camping in BC parks. However, if you have children to entertain, Shuswap Lake, with its warm summer days and fantastic beach, comes highly recommended. When we last visited, there seemed to be a number of parents looking after highly contented but energetic children who ran, cycled, played, and made new friends around the campsite. I am sure all these children will grow up remembering the summers of their childhood as always idyllic, and I felt quite jealous of their unadulterated enthusiasm and joie de vivre. For those who want to experience the delights of Shuswap Lake from a quieter vantage point, Herald (which caters more to the older camper) and Silver Beach provincial parks provide more tranquil alternatives.

→ Ellison Provincial Park

The soft, peach-coloured sand at Ellison is delightful.

F amous for having Canada's only freshwater dive park, Ellison must also rank as one of the best campgrounds in the Okanagan, primarily because it does not feel as busy as many of the others in the region and therefore offers a quieter family camping experience. Although only 16 kilometres away from a major population centre, it does not suffer from the constant hum of traffic as other popular parks in the Okanagan do (e.g., Haynes Point, Okanagan Lake). It is nestled in a Douglas fir and ponderosa pine forest on the northeastern shore of Okanagan Lake in one of the warmest areas of the province, which makes it easy to see why campers return here for a week or more at a time. Every age group can enjoy this idyllic spot from April to October.

History

This area owes its development to a man named Cornelius O'Keefe, who in the nineteenth century, while driving cattle from Oregon to the hungry men in the gold-mining areas of the Cariboo, discovered fertile grassland at the north end of Okanagan Lake. He decided not to drive cattle anymore, but to raise them in this location. He built a ranch, which still exists today (see *Rainy-day activities*). In 1962, more than a hundred years after O'Keefe first travelled the area, Ellison Provincial Park was created.

Location

This provincial park is located 16 kilometres south of Vernon on the northeast shore of Okanagan Lake. Signposts in Vernon indicate how to get to Okanagan Landing Road, which takes you to the park. The road from Okanagan Landing follows the lakeside, twisting and turning past orchards, farms, and ranches that have been an integral part of the community for over a century. The park is situated in 200 hectares of forested benchland high above a shoreline of rocks, cliffs, beaches, scenic headlands, and tranquil coves. To the west are the rolling hills of the Thompson Plateau and to the east are the distant Monashee Mountains.

Facilities

The seventy-one gravel camping spots here are perfect. Some have views of the lake, a few have direct access to the adventure play area (try staying at number 71, 69, 66, or 64 for this), and all are spacious and private enough to accommodate even the largest RV. There are flush and pit toilets, water, and wood for sale, but there are no showers or a sani-station. The park is wheelchair accessible and reservations are accepted.

Recreational Activities

HIKING Six kilometres of easy, child-friendly hiking trails wind their way through the park. Paved trails, a little steep in places, lead from the campground to the beaches at South Cove and Otter Bay, and a third unpaved trail leads to a pet-friendly beach from campsite number 11. The popular Nature Trail Loop is a forty-minute walk where explorers may see Columbian ground squirrels and even porcupines, according to BC Parks literature. Interpretive signs are along this route.

FISHING For those without a boat, it is possible to catch carp, burbot, kokanee, Rocky Mountain whitefish, and large rainbow trout from the shoreline. However, those with access to the water are the true angling winners. Vernon's tourist board states there are over a hundred lakes in which to fish, all less than an hour's drive from the city, with Okanagan Lake being one of the longest.

BOATING/DIVING There is no boat launch in the park itself, but there is a public boat launch (signposted from the road) 6 kilometres north of the campground. Waterskiing, powerboats, and jet skiers are allowed on the lake; mooring buoys are provided in South Bay and Otter Bay. Otter Bay in Ellison is the home of Canada's only freshwater dive park. A number of objects and artifacts have been sunk here to attract fish and rubber-clad individuals. BC Parks says the area has "been enhanced to provide a variety of fish for snorkelling and scuba diving," but seems reluctant to specify how this enhancement has occurred. For those of us who do not wish to try the activity, this is a great place to "diver watch," especially at the end of the day, as night diving is popular.

FAMILY ACTIVITIES The three protected beach areas with soft, peach-coloured sand are ideal places for swimming, sandcastle construction, and sunbathing. A change house with cold, freshwater showers is situated between the two coves, Otter Bay and South Cove. The third swimming location is at Sandy Beach (the only beach that permits animals). The existence of three locations ensures you never feel crowded, even if hordes of Grade 3 schoolchildren arrive, as was the case when we stayed. During our visit, we found that a volleyball net had been set up by Otter Bay. After a busy day swimming and sunbathing, children can find further entertainment in the adventure playground or playing ball games on the manicured playing field. This field has an underground sprinkler system that looks like it should belong to an expensive Okanagan golf course rather than a BC provincial park. This grass is also home to a great many ground squirrels that run around and appear out of dozens of holes, ready to be chased by the overenthusiastic five-year-olds. One of the most popular pursuits is an evening of stargazing, as the clear Okanagan skies offer fantastic astronomical opportunities. The paved roads of the park are good cycling and rollerblading terrain.

RAINY-DAY ACTIVITIES The community of Vernon, the oldest town in the province's Interior, dating back to 1892, is only 16 kilometres away and offers many urban pursuits. These include a museum and archive, art gallery, golf and minigolf, waterslides, and leisure centres. At the historic O'Keefe Ranch, 12 kilometres north of Vernon, there are tours of the O'Keefe mansion, preserved and restored heritage buildings (including a picture-postcard church), a huge model railway display, tons of cowboy memorabilia, a picnic area, restaurant, and gift shop. There are also a number of farm animals, adding further authenticity to this 1867 ranch. Should you find babysitters for the kids, the Okanagan Springs Brewery in Vernon offers tours during the summer months.

Summary

When they were younger, our two boys loved this park, as we were lucky enough to secure a campsite next to the field and playground. First thing in the morning, they were up and out, playing with the friends they had made the previous evening. My three-year-old managed to befriend four 13-year-old girls, which was a wonderful babysitting treat for us. While we were free to enjoy the sunshine and a book, he was kept entertained by four surrogate mothers, while our four-year-old chased ground squirrels. Unlike many provincial parks that offer good family camping, Ellison is not large. It is very friendly and, in my opinion, offers better swimming than the Okanagan Lake or Haynes Point campgrounds and also has nicer beaches. This is my favourite campground in the Okanagan, and for children under the age of ten, it is paradise.

→ Bear Creek Provincial Park

When I think of Bear Creek I am reminded of one of the most aromatic experiences of my life. I first visited in early spring, on a hot day when the smell of the cottonwood trees, which extend through the campground to the beach, was mingling with the scent of fir and pine to create an aroma that almost made me dizzy. When we visited in late June 2003, my four-year-old commented on the fact it was snowing—the cottonwood trees were shedding their spores to such an extent we even had "snowball" fights.

Smell is not the only draw here. In addition to its aromatic qualities, this is a campground with a friendly feel, ideal for families and campers who want the outdoors experience without travelling too far from the hustle and bustle of life. While Bear Creek is in the busy Okanagan region, it is situated on a relatively quiet road. Although the city of Kelowna is clearly in view, if you look the other way, you can pretend it does not exist. Like the other campgrounds in the Okanagan, Bear Creek is extremely popular, so do not expect to find a spot easily in July or August, and you must consider reserving if you want a holiday here. Do consider visiting even if you do not have a reservation or an intention to camp, as it is a wonderful place for a picnic and walk.

History

The 167-hectare park was created in 1981. Prior to then, the S.M. Simpson Company had owned the land, as the shoreline was ideal for "booming," or storing, floating logs. The Simpson Company sold its interest to Crown Zellerbach Canada Ltd., and in 1981, the Devonian Group of Alberta helped the BC government purchase the land. Crown Zellerbach retains the right to continue booming, so floating logs, an integral part of the BC economy, are often seen in the water adjacent to the park (and a number of "escaped" logs provide floating fun for children). The quality of the creek's water was recognized many years ago by the Kelowna Brewing Company, which established a brewery nearby. Unfortunately this is no longer in existence, although occasionally old quart-sized beer bottles are found.

Location

Situated in the Central Okanagan Basin, Bear Creek (sometimes called Lambley Creek) is just 9 kilometres west of Kelowna on the western side of Okanagan Lake. You reach it via a paved access road. All services are available in Kelowna.

Facilities

The campground has 122 wonderful private spots. Paved roads ribbon throughout the park, making access easy for even the largest RV. Some of the sites have views of the bubbling creek, so campers can sleep to the sound of murmuring water; others are beside fantastic grassy areas, ideal for ball games. The campground is fully equipped with showers, flush and pit toilets, and access for the disabled. Reservations are accepted and strongly advised. A small concession for the sale of ice cream, candy bars, ice, and pop exists.

Recreational Activities

HIKING Although not long (a total of only 10 kilometres), the hiking trails around Bear Creek are delightful. Information on the campground notice board states the main Canyon Rim Trail takes one to two hours to complete, although I did it in forty minutes, including stops for photographs of the lake, waterfalls, and gorge (not really recommended if your children are under five). It is quite steep in places, but worth the effort, with many opportunities to photograph the rushing water of Bear Creek. Interpretative boards along the route give information on the fauna and flora of the area, and if you are fortunate enough to hike this trail in spring, you will see and smell a stunning array of wildflowers. For those with less stamina, the Mid Canyon Trail also grants access to some spectacular views, especially from the aptly named "Steep and Deep Canyon" lookout.

The steep hiking trail near the gorge at Bear Creek is not recommended for children under five.

CYCLING The paved roads of the campground are cycling and roller-blading terrain.

FISHING Anglers catch rainbow trout, kokanee, and whitefish.

BOATING Powerboats are permitted on the lake via the park's boat launch.

WILDLIFE VIEWING Ornithologists are drawn to the hawks, owls, and swallows that live in the vicinity. In May, you can hear tree frogs, while the summer nights bring a chorus of crickets. In the early fall, kokanee spawn in the lower water of the creek. Rattlesnakes and gopher snakes that live in the area look similar, with the main difference being that rattlesnakes are poisonous. (I'd advise staying away from both of them!) There are illustrations on the information boards near the park change house suggesting that you should travel to the Kelowna hospital if you are bitten. The small creek in the park is good for playing Poohsticks (a game featured in Winnie the Pooh that involves racing sticks down a river or stream) and for building small dams.

FAMILY ACTIVITIES This is a great place for children, with over four hundred metres of sandy beach from which to enjoy the calm, safe water. Sandcastles and moats are easily constructed here. As mentioned above, the numerous washed-up logs enhance the range of activities to be undertaken in and around the lake. Dozens of picnic tables are found in a large grassy area, and there is a change house, horseshoe pit, and adventure playground. Small deposits of placer gold can be found in the creek, so remember to bring the gold pan and a lot of patience.

RAINY-DAY ACTIVITIES It is difficult to imagine a rainy day in the Okanagan, but if you do have the misfortune to experience bad weather, the rapidly growing city of Kelowna (a name derived from the Okanagan First Nation's word for grizzly bear) has a number of commercial activities, including an excellent kids' park (including a water park), open from 9:00 a.m. to 9:00 p.m. during July and August, go-karts, paintball, an exotic butterfly garden, orchards with guided tours, golf courses, and, of course, wineries. Even if the weather is really bad, the park's proximity to Kelowna means there is always something to do. There is an old paddlewheeler that sails past the campground and offers tours of the lake. It departs from Kelowna City Park, adjacent to the Ogopogo statue, which you (or your children) may wish to climb. Fintry Provincial Park, north of Bear Creek, is also well worth a visit and has lots of pleasant walks. Lake Okanagan Resort (a ten-minute drive north of Bear Creek) offers horseback riding and jet ski rentals.

Summary

When travelling in this area, be sure to keep an eye out for the legendary Ogopogo, a lake serpent said to inhabit the water of Okanagan Lake. Aboriginal people call it *N'ha-a-itk* meaning "spiritually powerful in water." The best viewing spot is reported to be south of Bear

Creek on the eastern side of the lake, 6 kilometres north of Okanagan Lake Provincial Park. It is believed BC's answer to the Loch Ness Monster makes its home in an underwater cave in this region of the lake. If there is no accommodation upon your arrival at Bear Creek, consider camping in Fintry, which has all the services that Bear Creek has (except the concession) and is larger and quieter with two lakeside swimming spots. Bear Creek is my second-favourite camping spot in the Okanagan. It's larger than Ellison and therefore not so intimate, but it is so convenient to everything in Kelowna. Its location makes it an extremely popular provincial park, so if you're planning a trip in July or August, make sure you have a reservation.

An impromptu game of volleyball beside the lake looks like a lot of fun.

→ Okanagan Lake Provincial Park

This tranquil scene is in the northern campground at Okanagan Lake Provincial Park.

I have to admit that before I had children, I did not care much for the Okanagan, regarding it as too populated, too barren, and too hot. How opinions change. Now I like the convenience of doughnut shops, coffee shops, and fast food outlets, love the warm temperatures in the shoulder camping months, and appreciate the vast array of services. Okanagan Lake Provincial Park is not my own personal preference in this area of the province (I prefer Ellison and Bear Creek), but data from BC Parks confirm it is the most popular provincial park in the Okanagan, with over twenty thousand camping parties staying each year—so, what do I know? My biggest problem stems from the fact that it is located relatively near a busy road, so the noise of traffic is easily audible in some sections of the campground. Having said that, it does provide easy access to a central part of the Okanagan and has wonderful vegetation, superb facilities, excellent views, generally good weather, and a 1,000-metre beach that does not have the noise problem, so perhaps I am just too picky. This is a campground that does not give a get-away-from-it-all feeling, and in this respect it is similar to Haynes Point, just down the road (see next section), or Rathtrevor on Vancouver Island. It is a family-friendly campground.

History

The park was established in 1955 and is unique in its development. In the 1950s, more than 100,000 trees were planted on the barren, rocky hillside. Many of them were non-native ornamental trees such as Manitoba, silver, and Norway maples; Russian olive; Chinese elm; Lombardy poplar; and red, blue, and mountain ash. This eclectic collection, together with the natural stands of ponderosa pine and Douglas fir, provides a home to a rich variety of bird life (see *Wildlife Viewing*). Each year the park's popularity grows, as does that of the whole Shuswap–Okanagan region.

Location

Okanagan Lake is in the Okanagan Basin, 24 kilometres north of Penticton, between the wonderfully named communities of Peachland and Summerland. The campground is on 81 hectares of hillside between the highway and the lake.

Facilities

Okanagan Lake has two campgrounds, both equipped with showers and pit and flush toilets. There are 168 vehicle/tent spaces, 88 of them in the southern part of the campground, where the boat launch is located. Spaces in the southern campground range in desirability. Some have good views of the lake, but are quite close together; others have the benefit of privacy provided by vegetation, but are farther away from the lake. Those in the northern campground tend to be larger and more private. Situated on a hillside, higher sites are close to the road and experience traffic noise (but compensate by having excellent views), while others lower down the slope are quieter. The park is wheelchair accessible (and the disabled washroom is great for family showering). Reservations are taken and strongly advised. Both campgrounds maintain a lush green environment because of an excellent sprinkler system, but be careful where you leave precious items (or kids) as they could suddenly get soaked, as ours did at 8:00 a.m. while we were having breakfast at the picnic table.

Recreational Activities

HIKING A few small trails wind through the park between the campgrounds. A pleasant one-hour stroll can be taken along a lakefront on a sandy trail strewn with pine cones. Sections of the sandstone cliffs along this track have unfortunately been scarred by graffiti, but despite this eyesore, the route is flat, pretty, and quiet. When you take this walk, you can decide the best bit of beach on which to spend the rest of the day. This trail is also good for cycling.

FISHING There is good fishing for carp, burbot, kokanee, Rocky Mountain whitefish, and large rainbow trout. When we stayed here, we spent hours catching toe-biters with fishing nets bought from a dollar store in Kelowna.

BOATING A boat launch is situated at the southern campground, and all types of powerboats are permitted on the waters. This can mean that a quiet paddle with a toddler is ruined by the jet ski crowd.

WILDLIFE VIEWING The diverse collection of trees attracts a variety of bird life, including hummingbirds, cedar waxwings, quail, red-shafted flickers, western meadowlarks, and Lewis woodpeckers. Gopher snakes and rattlesnakes are also found in the area.

FAMILY ACTIVITIES With more than a kilometre of lakeside beach (the better sections are found nearer the northern campground) and access to what is supposed to be the warmest water in the country, it is not surprising this location is so popular for swimming, windsurfing, sailing, sunbathing, and picnicking. The beach is somewhat stony, so water shoes are advisable. I tried to swim at the north beach and had great difficulty getting in, as the stones under my feet were so slippery. Watch out as well for a steep drop-off. Additional recreational options include a volleyball net and swings at the south campground.

RAINY-DAY ACTIVITIES With such close proximity to centres of population, there is a wealth of things to do if it rains. Old McDonald's Farm is approximately 10 kilometres north on Highway 97, just after the other McDonald's, which, incidentally, has a play area. The Kettle Valley Railway in Summerland operates a quaint steam train over the summer months. It travels for about 10 kilometres through picturesque countryside. Each year this attraction seems to expand and employs some wonderful volunteers and enthusiasts who offer tons of information for the tourists. Just south of the campground, at Okanagan Falls, is a brilliant ice cream store with many flavours to choose from, and where even the child-sized cones are huge. They also sell homemade fudge and other goodies—well worth the trip.

Summary

Okanagan Lake is an ideal camping spot for campers with children who are looking for a safe lakeside beach, or for those who want to have a central base from which to explore the Okanagan. It is the most popular campground in the region, offering all amenities in a pleasant environment. It is also very busy and, in this respect, not to everyone's preference. During the summer, the temperatures in this region soar into the high thirties, remaining there for weeks. The climate is extremely hot and dry, so if you are considering travelling to this region, my advice would be to avoid the busiest and hottest months (July and August), if at all possible, and choose to vacation in May or September, when the weather is still good and the temperatures more bearable. These are, for me, the best times to visit this popular area of BC, especially as the trees are in blossom from mid-April until the end of May, and most of the fruit (apricots, cherries, peaches, plums, pears, apples, and grapes) is still available in September.

→ Haynes Point Provincial Park

Haynes Point is a unique spit jutting out into Osoyoos Lake.

I t is a great shame this campground in the heart of the Okanagan Basin is not larger, as it is an extremely popular location during the summer months; however, the climate ensures a pleasant stay for those who choose to visit in the spring and fall. I have to confess this is not my first choice because of its almost urban setting. That said, it is ideal for those who like the luxury of camping on a beach near a major centre of population, and if you have older children, it is perfect. The town of Osoyoos is within walking distance (although the 2-kilometre walk is not a good one). This advantage, together with the proximity of some of the Okanagan's finest vineyards and fruit farms, means that from June to November there are fruit and vegetable stands at the sides of the highways, ensuring succulent produce is readily available for the camper's table. The season starts in May when the roadside stands sell fresh asparagus, which can also be found growing wild in the park.

History

This small 13-hectare park was created in 1962 and is named after Judge John Carmichael Haynes, who came to Osoyoos (originally known as Sooyoos) in the nineteenth century and became a renowned legal authority and landowner. He brought law and order to the goldfields of Wild Horse Creek, near Cranbrook, before moving in 1860 to assist the Okanagan area's gold commissioner and customs collector during the Rock Creek gold rush. He was subsequently appointed to the Legislative Council of BC and became a county court judge. Haynes built a large house in Osoyoos and established a ranch to serve the demands of the Cariboo gold miners. He lived there until his death in 1888. Historically, Aboriginal people lived, hunted, and fished in the area; two archaeological sites in the park tell their story. North of the park is a sandspit over which Highway 3 runs. This route forms part of the famous Hudson's Bay fur trading trail and has been used for centuries by fur traders, explorers, and miners. Today, orchards and vineyards dominate the area, with tourism contributing a major part to the economy. Veterans who settled in Oliver after the First World War established the first orchards.

Location

This very popular campground on Osoyoos Lake is found at the southern end of the Okanagan River Valley, in the rain shadow of the Cascade Mountains, just 2 kilometres from the United States border and 2 kilometres from Osoyoos on Highway 97. The park encompasses a narrow sandspit formed by wave action that, together with a nearby marsh, juts out three-quarters of the way into Osoyoos Lake. Haynes Point is signposted from Osoyoos, although the signage near the park is not great, so be careful you don't miss the turn. All services are available in Osoyoos.

Facilities

It is little wonder this is a popular retreat, as all the forty-one gravel camping spots are located on the sandspit, with over half having direct access to the beach only a few metres away. While there is not extensive vegetation, the spots are widely spaced. There are both flush and pit toilets, but no sani-station or showers. The park is accessible by wheelchair. Reservations are accepted and advisable as this is a popular location with both locals and tourists. One person I met here informed me that the locals have names for all the different campsites, adding a homey feel to the campground.

Recreational Activities

HIKING A small trail leads through the marsh area of the park. Each time we visit, this trail seems to be under construction and is consequently getting longer and longer! It has great access to the wildlife-rich area. When the water is clear, you get excellent views from the trail of the lake's fish. This is a great kids' trail, as they can explore by themselves and not get lost.

CYCLING The paved circular road at the campground is good cycling/rollerblading terrain, and of course, it is only a short bike ride to the town.

FISHING The lake is reputed to be the warmest in the country, making it a haven for up to twenty different types of fish. Rainbow trout, whitefish, and largemouth bass are abundant. Some of these huge specimens can easily be seen from a wooden bridge that runs over the marsh area.

BOATING Access to the warm water of Okanagan Lake is one of the primary reasons people decide to come here; for boating enthusiasts, the lake is perfect. The campground has a boat launch, and all types of powerboats and recreational craft are permitted on the lake, which regularly gets busy with windsurfers, paddlers, and powerboat operators. Expect noise from the jet ski set as well.

WILDLIFE VIEWING Those interested in wildlife may be rewarded by seeing the calliope hummingbird, Canada's smallest bird, as well as orioles, eastern kingbirds, and California quail. In the marsh area of the park, visitors may see canyon wrens and white-throated swifts. Other unusual creatures found in the area include spadefoot toads, painted turtles, rattlesnakes, and burrowing owls. Information boards at the park entrance give details about the appearance and habits of these animals.

FAMILY ACTIVITIES While adults enjoy this facility during the shoulder seasons, at other times it is primarily geared to those who have young children. Easy access to the safe water of the lake, coupled with the excellent climate of the region, means many happy families need look no farther than the sun and gravelly sand provided at Haynes Point. For those who just visit for the day, a change house is available in the day-use area. The paved circular road is good cycling/rollerblading terrain, and of course, it is only a short bike ride to the town. The lake can also easily be accessed from the town of Osoyoos, where the beach is sandier and where ice cream is abundantly available.

RAINY-DAY ACTIVITIES As mentioned above, only 2 kilometres away is the town of Osoyoos. A Spanish theme predominates here, with many stucco buildings and red-tiled roofs. A small museum is one of the town's few tourist attractions. Originally an 1891 log schoolhouse, it has a mixture of displays on topics including the history of irrigation, the history of BC's provincial police force (long since replaced by the RCMP), bird specimens, and Aboriginal artifacts. Osoyoos is the fruit capital of Canada. The season starts in June with cherries, followed by apricots, peaches, plums, apples, and grapes. The area also has Canada's only banana farm and must contain the highest number of fruit stands anywhere in the country. The warm climate and lack of rain promote desert plants such as ponderosa pine, bear cacti, sagebrush, and grease-wood. Just south of Oliver is a federal ecological reserve—a "pocket desert." It may be difficult to find, but once we discovered it, we found the area fascinating (desert.org). It supports subtropical flora and fauna such as cacti, horned lizards, rattlesnakes, and burrowing owls. Wear good shoes to explore the area.

Summary

If you want to be sure of sun, sand, and people during your summer vacation, make sure you book Haynes Point well in advance, as this campground is frequently full. It is one of very few provincial parks that restricts reservations to seven nights, not fourteen. It is a place for families, boaters, or people who just want to sit by a lake and watch others for the day. Haynes Point is not a place to visit if you want seclusion or quiet. One of the biggest disadvantages is that traffic noise or music from the nearby town can be easily heard. If you plan to stay in the summer months, be warned that the temperatures can be very hot for weeks, so pack the sunscreen. I think this campground is most suitable for parents with school-aged children, as it's small enough to let them run off and explore by themselves and gain independence without getting lost. The other real advantage here is the campground's proximity to the town, which has a number of fast-food options, so you don't always have to figure out what to barbecue for supper.

The view is idyllic from this picturesque camping spot.

→ Kikomun Creek Provincial Park

Kikomun Creek feels like an English country estate.

This is an excellent place for family camping if ever there was one. This campground feels to me like an English country estate with its large open grasslands. A number of quiet paved roads take you to locations in different regions of the park: the day-use area at Surveyors Lake, the main Surveyors Campground, the group camping area, South Pond Campground, the boat launch, and Koocanusa Reservoir. These different attractions and facilities are not closely packed together but are kilometres apart. The park consequently feels huge—much larger than its 682 hectares—just because you see so much of it as you go from place to place. This gives it quite a different feel compared to other provincial parks.

History

The park was established in 1972 to provide facilities for recreationists as well as to preserve an example of ponderosa pine/grassland habitat. The productive grasslands in and around the park were used initially by the Ktunaxa people, who hunted deer, moose, mountain sheep, goats, geese, and grouse, and then by the European settlers who set up cattle ranches. The Ktunaxa people named the creek 'Qikmin, a name that referred to its tendency to dry up or shrink in the summer months. The construction of the Libby Dam in Montana created the huge reservoir.

Location

Kikomun Creek is situated in the southern region of the Rocky Mountain Trench, 68 kilometres from Cranbrook. Turn off Highway 3/93 at Elko, 32 kilometres west of Fernie, and take the paved road 11 kilometres south. Some services are available at Jaffray, 11 kilometres from the park, but the nearest are at a private marina 4 kilometres from the park's entrance. The marina supplies gas, propane, fast foods, and has a grocery store.

Facilities

This campground was recently expanded and now offers 168 sites in three distinct locations. In my opinion, by far the best location is Surveyors Campground, a large campground with every amenity—including reservable sites, wheelchair accessibility, and showers—and spaces that can accommodate either the largest RV or smallest tent (tent pads available). Because of the sparse vegetation, many of these spaces feel quite open, but they are far enough apart to be completely private. This campground is on two levels, close to two sandy beaches. The second campground, Ponderosa, is also fully reservable with a new shower block. It provides a regimented line of spaces with no privacy, although a large grassy area nearby invites you to pitch your tent. This campground is close to the reservoir. The third location is Kalispell, which operates on a first-come, first-served basis. Only the basic facilities exist at this site. Choose these latter two campgrounds if boating is your primary passion, but be advised they not at all kid-friendly. There is a sani-station at the main entrance to the park.

Recreational Activities

HIKING There are a number of easy hikes you can take here. Surveyors Lake Trail is an easy forty-five-minute walk around the lake. Watch for painted turtles. Hidden Lake is a shorter thirty-minute interpretative stroll, while the Great Northern Rail Trail is a route for both mountain bikers and walkers (one to three hours depending on your mode of transportation, age, and level of fitness). Hikers of every age group can complete all trails. The first two feature interpretative boards along the route, while the latter is the subject of a leaflet you can collect from the campground host (if there is one) or at the start of the trail in Surveyors Campground.

CYCLING The park is perfect to cycle in, as there are not only quiet paved roads between the various campgrounds and day-use areas, but also a number of old roads and disused railway beds nearby. As mentioned above, the Great Northern Rail Trail is open to mountain bikers.

FISHING The six lakes here—Surveyors, Hidden, Engineers, Skunk, Fisher, Muskrat, and Koocanusa—all have fishing opportunities. Lake Koocanusa is noted for kokanee, Rocky Mountain whitefish, cutthroat trout, and Dolly Varden, while smallmouth bass, eastern brook trout, and rainbow trout are more prevalent in the smaller lakes. During the fall, kokanee spawn in Kikomun Creek.

BOATING A concrete boat launch is provided at Lake Koocanusa. Powerboats are prohibited on the smaller lakes. Boat rentals are available in the park.

WILDLIFE VIEWING The park is home to one of BC's largest populations of western painted turtles, so-called because of the bright pattern they exhibit underneath their shell. A wander around Surveyors Lake when the sun is out affords numerous opportunities to view these creatures soaking up the rays, while on a dull day their small faces can be seen bobbing in the water. Spotting these creatures can keep little ones entertained for hours. Interpretative boards around the lake pro-

A boat-launch campground overlooks Koocanusa Reservoir.

vide interesting facts about these cute reptiles. Badgers, elk, black and grizzly bears, coyotes, cougars, and deer all inhabit the region. Birds seen in the park include osprey, mallards, red-tailed hawks, bald eagles, owls, and American kestrels.

FAMILY ACTIVITIES This is an ideal place to sojourn if you have children. There are two gorgeous sandy beaches by Surveyors Lake, and the water is clear, clean, and quite warm. Young ones can spend hours building sand-castles, playing in the sunshine, or swimming to the offshore raft. There is an adventure playground near campsite 37 in Surveyors Campground. We stayed in early June, and the water was easily warm enough to swim in for both adults and children. If you end up doing nothing else, you'll love the beaches.

RAINY-DAY ACTIVITIES Those who want to explore the local communi-ties have many interesting options. The town of Fernie, a forty-minute drive from the park, has an interesting historical downtown core with buildings dating back to the 1890s. While in Fernie, take the historical walking tour, then visit the restored railway station for refreshments. Mount Fernie Provincial Park, 2 kilometres west of the town, is a good location for a picnic and walk. To the north of Kikomun is Fort Steele, which is well worth a visit whether you have children or not. This late-nineteenth century settlement was almost a ghost town until the 1960s, when the government recognized its potential as a heritage site. Today almost sixty structures have been restored, including the North West Mounted Police camp (where children will be entertained climbing up to the fort's lookout tower), a huge water wheel, printing office, hotel, and bakery complete with delicious home-baked treats. It's a fascinating place, made even more interesting by the presence of guides in period costumes and the fact it's still a work in progress, with some buildings under renovation or about to be renovated. Finally, the Kootenay Trout Hatchery on the Bull River, a thirty-minute drive from the park, is a fascinating place to learn about the trout-rearing process. Forty percent of the trout needed to stock BC lakes are reared here.

Summary

We stayed here without children one hot weekday in early June when at 6:00 p.m. it was still warm enough to swim in the lake—which we had to ourselves, watched by a noisy osprey who had built a nest in a tree overlooking the water. Four years later, we returned with kids in tow, and I was sure it wouldn't live up to my memories. But it did, and we've been back more recently to enjoy the updates that have occurred at this provincial park. I really appreciate the many things to do near the park. Don't miss Fort Steele. You can easily spend a day there, and it's a fantastic space for kids of any age to run around and explore.

→ Kokanee Creek Provincial Park

I t is rare to find a negative comment about Kokanee Creek Provincial Park. Some campgrounds are in fantastic locations, but away from major centres of activity, so campers must bring their own entertainment; others have little to offer in their own environment, but are conveniently situated for exploration of the surrounding area. Kokanee Creek provides hundreds of activities both within its boundaries and in its immediate area. And its huge, white, sandy beach makes it one of the best lakeside campgrounds in the province. It is easy to spend two weeks here and not run out of things to do, even if it rains.

Kokanee Creek is the centre of the kokanee salmon spawning activity, which takes place in late August and September. When we first stayed one September, it was not just the bright red salmon that were putting on a show. Their performance in the water was surpassed by a couple of ospreys who circled overhead, then dove into the waters of the creek only a few feet away from our vantage point, precariously flying away with huge salmon in their beaks. The spectacle was straight out of a *National Geographic* television program, although it is sad that a few of these fish, which have travelled so far just to spawn, will meet their demise so close to their destination. The area is noted for having one of the highest osprey populations in North America.

History

Kokanee means "red fish" in the Ktunaxa language, and it is the name given to the freshwater salmon that spawn in large numbers in the area. First Nations people inhabited the area many years ago and harvested these fish for the winter. At the beginning of the twentieth century, the region became popular with newcomers as gold and silver deposits were found in the surrounding hills and creeks. Legends tell of prospectors with names such as "Dirty Face Johnson" and "Dutch Charlie" who explored the area in search of precious metals. This exploration led to the development of some sizeable towns such as Nelson. Kokanee Creek Provincial Park was created in 1955.

Location

Kokanee Creek is in the Kootenay area of the province—an area often overlooked by tourists, who prefer to vacation in the Rockies or on the coast. This means the region is generally quieter than others, a real advantage if you choose to travel in the summer. The provincial park is set in the beautiful scenery of the Slocan Range of the Selkirk Mountains, on the western arm of massive Kootenay Lake, 19 kilometres north of Nelson on Highway 3. Services are conveniently located in Nelson or Balfour (12 kilometres to the south).

Facilities

Kokanee Creek provides 169 wooded camping spots in three locations: Sandspit (112 spaces), Redfish (19 spaces), and Friends (38 spaces). Redfish is close to the road, making Sandspit my personal preference. Sandspit may also be preferable for campers with kids as it is nearer the beach and playground, with a few sites overlooking the playground, and it does not entail crossing a main road to get to the beach. Kokanee Creek is home to the West Kootenay Visitor Centre, so the facilities here are good, including flush toilets, a sani-station, and disabled access. There are coin-operated showers, and a small number of sites at Friends have power. Reservations are accepted. The camping spots themselves are large enough to accommodate every type of recreational vehicle, and group camping is also available.

Recreational Activities

HIKING There are a number of small (twenty- to sixty-minute) trails that zigzag around the park, taking explorers to views of the spawning channels and to the beach. For those who demand a more serious stretch of the legs, Kokanee Glacier Provincial Park is a 32,000-hectare area with an extensive trail system. A leaflet describing these hikes is available from the visitor centre.

CYCLING The numerous paved roads in the campground are great for cycling and rollerblading.

FISHING The fishing here is reputed to be second to none for both rainbow trout and kokanee, and the locals claim that the world's largest rainbow trout (4.5 kilograms) was landed here. Dolly Varden, char, burbot, and whitefish are also regularly taken from the lake and nearby waterways. There are also, of course, ample opportunities for your children to use their nets and try for toe-biters in the many small streams.

BOATING The campground is equipped with a boat launch, and the lake is popular with kayakers, jet skiers, canoeists, powerboaters, water skiers, and windsurfers. Fortunately its huge area means it never gets crowded, although the noise of the jet skiers can be irritating if you are planning a quiet time on the beach.

FAMILY ACTIVITIES This provincial park is a delight for anyone with children, who will not want to return home from this paradise. There are a number of beautiful long sandy beaches and a safe swimming area, changing rooms, picnic facilities, and children's play area. The visitor centre has displays on salmon spawning, and when we visited one June, it had a live-bear trap on display outside.

RAINY-DAY ACTIVITIES One of the joys of staying here is the number of activities to do and sights to see close at hand—pursuits suitable for every taste and every age group. The community of Nelson is one of the oldest and certainly one of the prettiest in BC, with the highest concentration of heritage buildings in the province. In Nelson you can visit the museum, take a self-guided walking tour, or use the excellent indoor swimming pool.

Kaslo, 50 kilometres to the north, is a small community with a nine-hole golf course, coffee shops and cafés, and the SS *Moyie*, the last sternwheeler on Kootenay Lake, which is now a museum. For those interested in ghost towns and early prospecting history, Sandon, farther west along Highway 31A, is a delight to visit. It is slowly being renovated by a number of dedicated volunteers. When we visited, a gangly fourteen-year-old youth enthusiastically showed us the hydroelectric power room, complete with huge generators brought across from Manchester, England. There was also a teashop for refreshments and a souvenir store. The museum is highly recommended, and the town site is a great place for kids of any age to explore.

Ainsworth Hot Springs, 29 kilometres north of the park, boasts warm, therapeutic mineral pools and a system of caves stretching into the rock face to explore. (Go to hotnaturally.com to learn more.) When our kids were younger, they found the cave experience "too spooky," but loved the hot pools. The hot springs were completely renovated in 1998 and make a great place to visit even if the weather is bad. Cody Caves Provincial Park (no camping facilities) is located in the Selkirk Mountains above Ainsworth Hot Springs, just 11 kilometres along a good forest road off Highway 31. Visitors to the park can view spectacular cave formations including stalagmites, stalactites, waterfalls, draperies, rimstone dams, and soda straws. You are provided with the necessary protective clothing and hard hats when you take the highly informative tours offered by BC Parks, although these tours are not recommended for kids under seven years old.

What used to be the longest free ferry ride in the world, across Kootenay Lake from Balfour to Kootenay Bay, is just a twenty-minute drive north from the campground. If you have the opportunity, take a morning ferry and have breakfast—the trip is entertaining and the price is unbeatable.

Summary

If you are searching for a campground where you can pitch a tent for a week or more, and which offers swimming, sunbathing, and water sports in addition to numerous other activities within an hour's drive, then look no farther than Kokanee Creek. It is an idyllic family lakeside location. One of the times I enjoy most is dusk, when the day trippers are gone and there are quiet trails to walk on while I watch the sun go down and the stars come out. For those of us who live in the Lower Mainland or Alberta, the nine-hour plus drive to the Kootenays may be off-putting, but it is well worth it. In addition to the camping, I regard the town of Nelson as the most beautiful in the province. We stayed at Kokanee Creek with our two young children late one September, when most of the sites had been closed, picnic tables were stacked ready for storage, and there was no one to collect our fee. We had to wear fleece to explore the campground comfortably and take walks, but the place was all ours, so it remains very special to us.

→ Kootenay National Park

Kootenay National Park is another campground that offers mountain scenery and where nearby hot springs can be found in the Rockies. This park appeals to both adults and children. While the adults may be most struck by the spectacular scenery and wildlife, the kids will love the hot springs and the various small walks that can be easily completed. During my first visit to Kootenay National Park, I met a parks representative who told me that Kootenay was often overlooked in comparison to its well-known neigh-

A footbridge crosses over Marble Canyon.

bours, Banff and Jasper. For anyone who has experienced the crowds at Lake Louise or Banff in August, this can only be good news. Kootenay's 140,600 hectares are rich in variety. It is the only park to contain both glacial peaks and cacti within its boundary; but these are not the only rewards. Radium Hot Springs, numerous gorges, waterfalls, mountains, and two major river systems (the Vermilion and the Kootenay) add to its glory, as do a host of interesting excursions for the tourist. In 1985, UNESCO designated Banff, Jasper, Yoho, and Kootenay National Parks as

World Heritage Sites, officially recognizing the beauty and significance of the Rocky Mountains and creating one of the largest protected mountainous areas in the world.

History

Interpretative boards at Marble Canyon detail the area's 500-million-year-old geological development. Human habitation is a little more contemporary, but it still goes back a long way. Aboriginal people have travelled, hunted, and camped in the region for over eleven thousand years. They recognized the magic of the hot springs and regarded them as sacred waters, a place to cure illness and gain spiritual peace. The first registered owner of the hot springs was Roland Stuart, an Englishman who purchased 65 hectares of land, including the hot springs, for $160 in the first decade of the 1900s. The government of Canada expropriated the land and springs from Stuart in 1923 and has been responsible for them ever since. Kootenay National Park opened in 1920 and owes its birth to Highway 93, the first road to cross the central Canadian Rockies, which in turn led to the development of motorized tourism. The province of BC gave the park to the government of Canada in return for the road.

Location

The park encompasses land of the Continental Divide and the Columbia Valley. The west entrance is 1 kilometre north of Radium, and the park stretches along 90 kilometres of Highway 93 as it heads north. All services can be found at Radium, and there is also a restaurant, store, and information office at Vermilion Crossing, operated by Kootenay Park Lodge and located roughly in the centre of the park.

Facilities

Three campgrounds operate within the park's boundaries. The largest and most popular is Redstreak, which is open from early May until the end of September and has 242 sites, including 50 with full hookup and 38 with electricity. There are also TENTik's—pre-erected tents—to rent at this location. Flush toilets, showers, and a sani-station are available here, as are facilities for the disabled. Redstreak is my personal preference as not only does it have all amenities, but also it is possible to walk to the hot springs from here (about fifteen minutes). This campground is not signposted very well; you enter it by exiting the park and taking a paved road beside the RCMP station in Radium on Highway 93/95. Stay here if you want easy access to the hot waters.

McLeod Meadows Campground is open from mid-June until mid-September and is 26 kilometres north of Radium between Meadow Creek and Kootenay River. It has ninety-eight spaces, flush toilets, a sani-station, but no showers. The spaces are large enough for every size of RV and are in a lightly forested area, with some of the best locations being close to the river. The third campground is Marble Canyon, open from mid-June until early September, 86 kilometres north of Radium. With sixty-one spaces set in a dense, subalpine forest, it is the quaintest of the campgrounds, and it has flush toilets and a sani-station but no showers.

Recreational Activities

HOT SPRINGS Radium Hot Springs are probably BC's best known hot springs and among the most developed. They are also the most radioactive hot springs in Canada, but don't worry—this radioactivity is too weak to be harmful. The pools are immensely popular; over 400,000 people use the facilities each year. There are two developed open-air pools: a hot soaking pool with temperatures up to 47.7 degrees Celsius, and a cooler swimming pool, 24 metres long, with hot water cooled by creek water to 27 degrees Celsius. The smaller, hotter pool nestles into the walls of the cliff, and it is possible to look up to see bighorn sheep on the ledges above the pool. You can access the pools via a trail from Redstreak Campground or by vehicle. The hot springs are very popular, especially during the summer. When we visited in July, we found that opening time (9:00 a.m.) was a good time to go to avoid the crowds. For those who arrive unprepared, locker rooms, showers, and swimsuit and towel rentals

The pools at Radium Hot Springs are immensely popular.

are all available. This is a great place for kids of every age and fully accessible for the disabled.

HIKING One of the joys of Kootenay Park is the number of short, easy, yet fascinating trails that can be undertaken by any age group. Among the most popular are the following: Olive Lake, a boardwalk trail with interpretative signboards and a fish-viewing platform, 13 kilometres from Radium; Paint Pots (85 kilometres north of Radium), a 1.5-kilometre trail leading to cold, iron-laced mineral springs that bubble up through the earth and stain it a deep ochre colour; and Marble Canyon, a kilometre-long interpretative trail, easily completed with young children, through an impressive narrow canyon of grey limestone that leads to a pounding waterfall. There are over 200 kilometres of trails in the park, so numerous day hikes are possible in addition to overnight excursions. One of the most popular day hikes is a 10-kilometre trek (about a five-hour return trip) to Stanley Glacier through a dramatic landscape of fire and ice. Details of all these routes can be obtained from the park information centre, 3 kilometres north of Radium, or at the Vermilion Crossing visitor centre, 63 kilometres north of Radium.

FISHING While it is possible to fish for brook and rainbow trout, whitefish, and Dolly Varden, most of the streams and rivers are fed by glaciers, so the water is too cold to yield high fish populations.

BOATING Only non-motorized craft are permitted on the lakes and rivers in the park.

WILDLIFE VIEWING In addition to 179 species of birds found in the park, Kootenay is home to grizzly bears, black bears, wolves, elk, moose, bighorn sheep, and mountain goats. The best time to see these creatures is in the early morning and at dusk.

FAMILY ACTIVITIES With no developed beach or natural waterfront, Kootenay is not a prime family location if your children are very young. However, Redstreak Campground does provide easy access to the hot springs and pool, has an adventure playground, and is near to the town of Radium, so if you have children to entertain, there is plenty to do. The numerous short trails scattered throughout the park are easy for children to complete and are immensely educational. Lake Windermere, a fifteen-minute drive south of Kootenay National Park, has two lovely beaches and relatively warm water, and is easily accessible from James Chabot Provincial Park (no camping), so if your children want water-based activities, head there.

RAINY-DAY ACTIVITIES The communities of Radium and Invermere offer a number of commercial activities, including golf. Radium has a number of restaurants and fast-food outlets. Invermere is a pretty town whose main street is lined with flowers in the summer. If you have not had enough of hot pools, head farther south to check out Fairmont Hot Springs, which has a restaurant and lots of grass for the kids to play on, and has seen considerable development over the last few years.

Summary

For me, there are two sides to Kootenay National Park. The southern portion near Radium is busy and somewhat commercialized. During the summer, it is crowded as tourists congregate around the thera-peutic waters of the hot springs. The other side of Kootenay is its vast expanse away from the hot waters, which provides a cornu-copia of things to see and do. It is easy to spend two to three days travelling slowly through the park, exploring its natural wonders, walking the trails, and camping at the different locations.

For those who want access to the hot springs but wish to retire to a quiet, small campground in the evenings, Dry Gulch Provincial Park is an interesting option. Five kilometres south of Radium on Highway 93/95, this little-known haven has twenty-six tranquil sites that, to my eye, are superior to those at Redstreak. There are no showers or hookups, and access to the hot springs requires a drive, but it is a more private campground.

Olive Lake from the boardwalk trail.

PART 3

Western Alberta

→ Waterton Lakes National Park

The family pauses to admire the view in Waterton Lakes National Park.

T he first time I visited Waterton, the weather was not brilliant, but as we arrived and took our first steps to the visitor centre, a red fox casually meandered up the adjacent path toward the women's washrooms, just as two women emerged. They were as surprised by the four-footed visitor as we were. From this initial encounter, I knew Waterton was special. My children expected Little Bear and his animal friends to be around the next corner! Compared to Jasper and Banff National Parks, Waterton is not as large and is somewhat out of the way. It is much quieter, but just as spectacular. The town of Waterton is *much* less crowded than Banff, Jasper, or Lake Louise, and is consequently a far more pleasant environment in which to spend time. This is a national park for every age group, and with the majestic Prince of Wales Hotel dominating the skyline, this is one where I definitely plan to return to one day without kids.

History

Waterton became Canada's fourth national park in 1895, ten years after the first national park was established at Banff. It meets Montana's Glacier National Park at the border of United States and Canada; in 1932, both were designated as the world's first International Peace Park, acknowledging the bonds of peace and friendship between the two countries. In 1995, the two parks were given World Heritage Site designation because of the glacier-carved landscapes, more than twelve hundred species of plants and animals living within the boundaries, and the rich biological diversity. The elegant Prince of Wales Hotel, reputed to be one of the most photographed hotels in Canada, was built in 1926 by the Great Northern Railway's president, Louis Hill, and it retains much of its 1920s charm (which, of course, is lost on any under-five you take there).

Location

Waterton Lakes National Park is located in the southwest corner of Alberta, 264 kilometres from Calgary, and 130 kilometres from

Lethbridge. It is a relatively small 50,000-hectare park, but in that space there is more plant and animal life than in Banff and Jasper combined (960 species of plants, 250 species of birds, and over 60 mammals).

Facilities

There are three primary campgrounds at Waterton. The main Waterton Township Campground, open May to October, is the only one with showers and is located in the town. It is *very* open and can get somewhat windy. While it accommodates all sizes of RVs and tents (238 spaces), the openness offers little privacy and there are no individual firepits. If you want to be near the cappuccino bars or restaurants, it is the place to be. We stayed at Crandell Mountain, which was fantastic and had large sites and excellent views; it offered no showers but had well-kept bathrooms with flush toilets and sinks. There are 129 spaces here, and it's ideal for kids of any age as there is so much to explore in the surrounding undergrowth or by cycling on the gravel roads. Similarly, Belly River Campground offers the same type of camping experience, but is much smaller (24 spaces) and pretty rustic. Reservations are accepted at township by going online (reservation. pc.gc.ca) or by calling 1-877-737-3783.

Recreational Activities

HIKING The park boasts more than 200 kilometres of trails, and what we really appreciated was the number of trails that were easily accessible; they were not lengthy, but interesting nevertheless. From the visitor centre, try the 1.2-kilometre climb up Bears Hump Trail— well worth it for the views of the lakes (but not advised for very young children). The Linnet Lake Loop Path is wheelchair accessible, so it's ideal if your offspring are in a stroller. This trail offers lots of interpretive information along the way. Our kids really enjoyed the Red Rock Canyon Trail (easily completed by a three-year-old) and the 1-kilometre return walk to Blackiston Falls through a forest with evidence of bear scat and across bridges ideal for playing Poohsticks.

Scenic Blackiston Falls in Waterton Lakes National Park are easily accessible.

When you get to Blackiston Falls, you will find wonderful photo opportunities. There are also a number of far more strenuous hikes. Free trail information is given at the visitor centre, which also offers guided hikes.

CYCLING Bikes are available for rent in the town of Waterton (including those large "family" bikes where two parents pedal a huge monstrosity without gears and the kids ride in style). The town itself is flat and easy to explore. Mountain biking in the park is limited to five trails.

FISHING For the family that fishes, cutthroat trout, rainbow trout, Arctic grayling, northern pike, and whitefish can all be caught.

BOATING For the young and the young at heart, canoes, kayaks, paddleboats, and rowboats can be rented at Cameron Lake from a very funky little outlet that also sells candy bars, coffee, and fishing supplies. Boating, waterskiing, and scuba diving are popular on Upper and

Middle Waterton lakes, but be warned—the water is cold so wetsuits are advised. Interpretive boat cruises, which have been in operation since 1927 and which take about two and a half hours, seem popular with visitors to Waterton but can be quite costly for a family.

WILDLIFE VIEWING More than a thousand species of plants and wildlife call Waterton Lakes National Park home. You will have various opportunities to see plenty of wildlife while exploring some of the trails or even just relaxing at your campsite.

FAMILY ACTIVITIES The town of Waterton has a fantastic golf course should your children be old enough to enjoy this sport, or, if they're at the other end of the scale, a playground with a water park is ideally situated opposite an ice cream store. Parks staff offer interpretive programs in the summer at the two main campgrounds, and during the peak summer months, a number of kids' programs are offered; check out the visitor centre when you arrive to find what's available. The town itself is a great place to wander and window shop, and there is a nice stroll on the Lakeshore Trail from Waterton. Geocaching for those with a GPS is offered. It is possible to swim in Upper Waterton Lake, but the lake is cold and subject to strong winds; consequently swimming is not a key activity here.

RAINY-DAY ACTIVITIES Unfortunately, you may really need this information, since Waterton is reputed to have Alberta's highest average annual precipitation (1,072 millimetres), with April, May, and June being the wettest months. As mentioned above, the Prince of Wales Hotel is well worth a visit and serves a wonderful high tea from June to September. There's a small movie theatre in town and a heritage museum. Although we stayed when it was rainy, we found one of the most enjoyable things to do with young kids was to take slow drives and stop at all the markers, get out, get wet exploring, and then move on. Canada's first oil well is situated in the park, as are a number of other spots of interest along Red Rock Canyon Road and Akamina Parkway. If you really need to escape the elements, drive for ninety minutes toward Lethbridge, and north of Fort Macleod on Highway 2, where you will find the Head-Smashed-In Buffalo Jump historic site. Here is a wonderful museum of First Nations' heritage that children and adults alike will find extremely stimulating and informative. The building itself is constructed into the rock. When you arrive at the entrance, three huge buffalo stare down on you. There is also an excellent theatre and a few small trails—a very kid-friendly place.

Summary

The disadvantage to Waterton Lakes National Park is that there is no beach or warm water, and if you stay for more than three days, you'll probably need to wear rain gear at some time. It is therefore a park more suitable for older children and teenagers. The advantages, though, are the spectacular scenery, brilliant wildlife, and gorgeous wildflowers that seem to dominate every hillside not covered with forest, a number of easy walks, and a lovely camping experience. Waterton is renowned as the place "where the mountains meet the prairies." The four main lakes—Lower, Middle, and Upper Waterton, and Cameron—can easily be accessed by car, and the roads provide ample opportunities for picnicking and exploring. Waterton Lakes National Park is a wonderful place to introduce your kids to a spectacular environment, and even if they do go home remembering only who found the largest slug, or whose Poohstick was the best flowing in the fast rivers, or, as in our case, where the plastic Batman toy was lost, you'll feel like your parental batteries have been recharged by camping in this remarkable park. If you desire to introduce your offspring to mountain biking, hiking, or just being outdoors in the elements, this park really does deliver the goods and you'll have the added bonus of doing it all among some breathtaking scenery.

→ Peter Lougheed Provincial Park

Peter Lougheed Provincial Park is located in beautiful Kananaskis Country.

One of the real joys of this provincial park, one of the largest in Alberta, is the choice of six vehicle-accessible campgrounds within its boundaries, all of which offer distinct camping experiences in Kananaskis Country. This is a park for those who love cycling and hiking, but it's also great for families as it offers a number of interpretive programs, has a gorgeous visitor centre and on-site services, and sits among snow-capped peaks, glacial streams, picture-postcard lakes, and wonderful forests—all within an hour's drive from Calgary.

History

Aboriginal people used the Kananaskis Valley for thousands of years as a hunting ground for bison, elk, and deer. The name Kananaskis derives from a legend of an Aboriginal man who received a very heavy blow to his head from an axe but then recovered. Upon hearing this legend,

John Palliser, an early explorer who visited the region in 1857, named the river Kananaskis; now Kananaskis is often translated as "meeting of the waters." In 1978, Alberta premier Peter Lougheed officially dedicated Kananaskis Country and Kananaskis Provincial Park. In 1986, the park was renamed Peter Lougheed Provincial Park in honour of the premier whose vision of a protected wilderness recreational area for Albertans led to its creation.

Location

The 50,800-hectare park is located in the centre of Kananaskis Country, 46 kilometres south of Highway 1 on Highway 40, about an hour's drive from Calgary. It is part of the Canadian Central Rockies. Peter Lougheed is one of a number of provincial parks that exists within Kananaskis Country; however, some others do not offer camping.

Facilities

Peter Lougheed has six vehicle campgrounds (as well as six backcountry campgrounds and two group campgrounds); almost 600 camping spaces exist for every size of vehicle. The most popular campgrounds (and the ones with showers) are Boulton (118 spaces) and Elkwood (130 spaces). These are also the campgrounds that offer interpretive programs in the evenings, and are the ones that are very popular and need to be reserved in advance. When we visited, we preferred to stay in the less crowded Lower Lake campground (104 spaces and playground), which had easy access to the lake. Canyon Campground (50 spaces) is farther away from the interpretive programs and the lake but has easy access to a scenic reservoir. When we stayed in late June on a weekday, this was the quietest campground, with only two spaces taken. Mount Sarrail (44 spaces) and Interlakes (48 spaces) are ideal if you want easy access to the lake and fishing opportunities. There is a small store and restaurant at Boulton. Campsites at Boulton and Elkwood can be reserved at reservealbertaparks.ca or by calling 1-877-537-2757. All campsites are large and, with the exception of some at Canyon, are in a forested environment.

Recreational Activities

HIKING As with all large provincial parks, there are trails to suit every need and ability. The visitor centre sells a leaflet that has all the routes and maps. There are a number of interpretive trails ideal for kids. Try Kananaskis Canyon, a 1-kilometre loop, or, for a really good view of a cirque and a geology lesson, try Black Prince Cirque, a 4.5-kilometre loop. Trail conditions can change, so its always a good idea to check the park website or call the visitor centre.

CYCLING This really is the place to be if you love cycling; there are more than 100 kilometres of bike trails and over 12 kilometres of paved bike trails. The paved track is ideal if your kids are riding behind in a trailer, but be warned—much of the paved track is not level. The best place to start your journey on the paved track is from the visitor centre. This trail then ribbons its way by Upper Kananaskis Lake and includes sections of the Lodgepole, Wheeler, and Lakeside Trails. If you need more of a challenge, try the 24-kilometre Smith-Dorrien Loop Trail. The visitor centre can provide maps and advice.

FISHING Although we didn't catch anything (or see anyone else catch anything), our dollar-store fishing tackle was put to good use in the lakes next to the campground during our after-dinner strolls. Brook, cutthroat, rainbow, and bull trout, as well as mountain whitefish can all be caught.

BOATING Boat launches are available at the day-use areas of Upper Lake and Canyon.

WILDLIFE VIEWING Kananaskis Country is home to many large animals, including grizzly bears, elk, moose, and deer.

FAMILY ACTIVITIES The visitor centre, with fantastic interactive displays and huge stuffed animals, is a delightful place for kids to explore. In addition to the displays, there is a lounge with huge picture windows overlooking a grassy meadow. As mentioned, the park offers a number of interpretive programs during the summer months. These often take the form of plays and skits, providing education through entertainment to every age group. There are two playgrounds in the campgrounds at Lower Lake and Boulton.

RAINY-DAY ACTIVITIES When we visited this park, it rained, so we headed off to explore Kananaskis Village. I had anticipated it to be a smaller version of Whistler or Jasper, but not at all. The only saving grace was the brand new "Tot Lot," a playground for kids, which was so unused we had to make three deer go away from the slide before our kids could use it. There was a small café and a post office, but little else to see or do. There is a famous golf course, reported to be one of the best in the world, should you decide to remortgage your house and play golf. To the north of the park, Boundary Ranch offers horseback riding excursions.

Summary

Although when we stayed, the weather wasn't great, my kids really loved the adventure that Peter Lougheed Provincial Park offered. Here they could safely wander from the campsite into the muddy, low-lying areas to discover secret trails. After toasting marshmallows one night, we went to the lake to look for moose and to fish; then the next night, we stayed up and went to the amphitheatre for a discussion on bears, complete with sound effects that had everyone in the audience enthralled. For the camper, Peter Lougheed Provincial Park offers six different venues to try, which translates to six different environments for your children to explore. It is this vast size and variety of sites, as well as the fact it is so close to Calgary, that makes camping here so popular with Albertans. But remember, it is the Rockies and sometimes the snow is slow to melt and quick to return.

→ William A. Switzer Provincial Park

Cloudy skies can't dampen the experience of this beautiful Alberta campground.

You heard it here first: avoid Jasper and Banff, especially during the peak summer months and head to the wonderful William A. Switzer Provincial Park, which is just up the road. Still in the Rockies with glacier lakes and wetlands, this 9,300-hectare park is a real gem and much quieter than its famous cousins. Alberta Parks literature states you are more likely to see creatures than humans when here because it has many of the characteristics of the famous national parks but is way quieter. This is a great place for a family camping excursion, and one blogger refers to this park as "the Swiss army knife of camping" as it has something for everyone.

History

From 1880 to 1920, a store and trading post operated here to enable trappers and travellers to purchase supplies. The park was established in 1958 and was originally called Entrance Provincial Park, after the town located at the railway entrance to Jasper National Park. In 1974, it was renamed after William A Switzer, a member of the Alberta legislative assembly.

Location

Just a twenty-minute drive from the town of Hinton, where all services are available, the park is located on Highway 40, the Bighorn Highway, north of Jasper. This is a popular route to Alaska and therefore patronized by a number of RVers. It is situated in the foothills of the Canadian Rockies at an elevation of 1,150 metres, approximately 300 kilometers west of Edmonton.

Facilities

There are five camping locations in the park. The largest and reservable ones are Gregg Lake and Lakeside, which supply all services including play parks, amphitheatre, flush toilets, coin-operated showers, and a sani-station. The Gregg Lake location is a little way from the lake itself but has 164 sites, including 40 with power. It is a huge, spacious campground. The best kid-oriented campground is Jarvis as this is closer to the beach, has a playground, and is more intimate (24 spaces). I was informed at certain times this section of the park resembles an elementary school field more than a campground as kids can outnumber adults by five to one. Quieter, more rustic unreservable spaces can be found at Cache (14 spaces) and Halfway or Graveyard (12 spaces each). I almost felt these sites should be reserved for adults, as they were detached from the main kid-centred attractions. All sites are large and forested, so unlike many other campgrounds in Alberta, shade is not a problem. Firewood is available, and reservations are a must during July and August.

Recreational Activities

HIKING There are a number of self-guided interpretive trails. The smaller ones leave from the visitor centre and can be completed by young children and by those in strollers or wheelchairs. The Jarvis Lake Trail is a great 10-kilometre loop suitable for families with older kids, while the 4-kilometre Gregg Lake Trail accommodates tinier feet. It is also well worth hiking up to the Athabasca Lookout to see the Soloman Valley from a height of 1,585 metres. In 2014, I was told that a number of longer trails were under construction.

CYCLING The Gregg Lake Trail and Jarvis Lake Trail are both open for bikes. It is possible to cycle between the two main campgrounds (Jarvis and Gregg Lake) on the highway, which is not that busy, or around the Gregg Lake Campground, which is huge.

FISHING Known as "Fish Lakes" by the locals—which should tell you something—the five lakes in the park are home to native whitefish and northern pike. There is a pond stocked with rainbow trout next to Cache Lake Road and another at pond Jarvis Creek stocked with brown trout.

BOATING Canoeists can experience the 4-kilometre interpretive canoe route, as Jarvis Lake interconnects a chain of five lakes in the park. In some years, private contractors offer canoe rentals in the park, but this service seems to be a little sporadic. You can water-ski on Jarvis Lake, and there are boat launches.

WILDLIFE VIEWING The wildlife here is abundant. There are grizzly bears, black bears, wolves, coyotes, cougars, moose, elk, beaver, and more than 150 species of birds, including bald eagles, hawks, loons, ospreys, great grey owls, and snipes.

FAMILY ACTIVITIES There is a great sandy beach and a cordoned-off swimming area at the Jarvis Lake day-use area. During the summer, this beach, with easy access to the clear lake water, is a magnet for kids. A smaller beach is found at the Gregg Lake day-use area, and there is also a *very* small beach adjacent to the visitor centre, which feels crowded with only ten bodies on it. Numerous play parks are available at the day-use areas and campgrounds. The visitor centre in the park offers interpretive programs in the amphitheatre and advice on what to do. They also give guided hikes. Their building houses a magnificent grizzly bear skin and a number of stuffed animals. It has a great view of the surrounding mountains and is the place to start and acquaint yourself upon arrival.

RAINY-DAY ACTIVITIES Hinton has a 25-metre pool, a kid pool, hot tub, and sauna, so if the weather is uncooperative, a great few hours can be spent at this leisure centre. A small forest service museum is

The visitor centre at William A. Switzer Provincial Park features fun and practical information about the wildlife and activities found in the park.

in the town, and at the time of writing, a historical centre was under construction. Hinton is also home to the Beaver Boardwalk. This 3-kilometre-long wooden path winds its way through a living wetland of beaver habitat and has interpretive signs and two lookouts. Evening is the best time to see beavers. Slightly farther afield, the Miette Hot Springs in Jasper National Park may not be the best kept, but they do have wonderful views and it's easy to pass a day sitting in them looking out at the mountains. Burgers and kid food are also available, and I understand it's a great place to get breakfast. A visit to Jasper is only 95 kilometers away, and from here you can experience Maligne Canyon or take the SkyTram for some amazing views. Farther north of the campground at Grande Cache (about a one-hour drive), kids of every age can enjoy whitewater rafting, paintball, and horseback riding.

Summary

Visit in July and experience a vast array of wonderful wildflowers. Remember, though, that visits during the shoulder seasons can be quite cold at night. If your ambition is to get the kids excited about outdoor adventures, then William A. Switzer is your place. It is a park for every age of child. Young kids will love the beach areas and prevalence of other children to make friends with. Older children will be stimulated by the hiking and canoeing opportunities, and parents can relax knowing that restaurants, pizza joints, and a hospital are only twenty minutes away at Hinton. Additionally, when I visited, I discovered the Canadian Forces School of Search and Rescue is situated close to Jarvis Lake, so if you do lose a child, you can relax knowing help is close at hand.

→ Aspen Beach Provincial Park

A tranquil spot for camping at Aspen Beach.

When I arrived at Aspen Beach, the first thing I saw was a rather dated motorhome with the word "happy" written on a small overhead window above the driver's and passenger's seats. "Happy" certainly describes the hoards of campers who visit this campground, the largest in Alberta. Aspen Beach is set on a "lake," but it really should be described as an ocean for it stretches out as far as the eye can see. Gull Lake has a total surface of 8,060 hecatres and a maximum depth of 8 metres. The park is within easy reach of Edmonton, Red Deer, and Calgary making it a very popular family camping location. Reservations are essential here, particularly in July and August, and on long weekends.

History

Created in 1932, Aspen Beach was Alberta's first provincial park. Homesteaders were the earliest settlers to the region, and they established themselves south and west of Gull Lake at the end of the nineteenth century. Many came from the United States. A steamboat was used on Gull Lake to aid the sawmill operations at Birch Bay at the same time.

Location

This campground is found 135 kilometres south of Edmonton and 27 kilometres northwest of Red Deer. It is therefore located about two hours from both Edmonton and Calgary, and just thirty minutes from Red Deer. The park covers only 214 hectares and is on the southwestern shore of Gull Lake, a very large shallow lake. Access is from Highway 12. It is 17 kilometres from the town of Lacombe. Six kilometres away, the community of Bentley has a number of restaurants, a large grocery store, small museum, gas station, and bars.

Facilities

There are two campgrounds, Lakeview and Brewers, in this park. As separate facilities, they offer services that vary considerably in size, location, and vegetation. Both have their own gatehouses to book in would-be tenants and are in two distinct locations (but connected by trails). Lakeview has 27 unserviced sites, 151 power sites, and 77 power-water-and-sewer sites. They are set out in quite a regimented way and can be quite expensive at forty-four dollars (unserviced are more reasonable at twenty-six dollars in 2014). Brewers Campground has 300 unserviced sites, which are more secluded and rustic and which have limited shade from adjacent bushes and boreal trees (this site is my preference). With over 550 camping spaces, Aspen Beach is the largest Alberta campground and much larger than any BC campground. Some of the sites are not as large as those found in other parks in this book and can be tightly packed. All sites have access to firepits, wood, pit and flush toilets, showers, and picnic tables. There is a small, cash-only concession serving hot dogs, candy, and hamburgers in the day-use area. Reservations are accepted and strongly advised. In addition to the two campgrounds, there is the Ebeling Beach day-use area, where an awesome beach is found.

Recreational Activities

HIKING Hiking is not a key pursuit here, although a number of trails do ribbon through the park.

CYCLING One of the best things to do here is cycle. A paved bike path leads from the campground to the town of Bentley, which can take you anywhere from twenty minutes to two hours to complete, depending on the age of your fellow cyclists. Red benches are provided along this route if a rest is required, and the route passes adjacent fields so is quite pretty. If you decide to ride to the town on Saturday afternoon, you will be rewarded by the vendors of a sweet little farmers market. A number of small trails and paths ribbon through the campground, some paved.

FISHING It is possible to fish for northern pike, burbot, lake white fish, lake sucker, yellow perch, and walleye in Gull Lake. Specific catch and size limits operate to preserve stocks. There is a neat pier.

BOATING Powerboats are permitted on this vast lake, so consequently many visitors water-ski. Windsurfing, canoeing, paddle-boarding, and kayaking are also popular. There is a boat launch at Lakeview Campground, but it's only suitable for smaller vessels. Life jackets are available for rent in the park, and there is a "Life Jacket Loaner Station" for children's jackets, although it was not well stocked when we visited.

WILDLIFE VIEWING The location attracts migratory waterfowl. A walkway around the marsh has viewing platforms to see these birds.

FAMILY ACTIVITIES The shallow, warm water, large expanse of beach, and play areas on the beach make this an ideal family location, especially for those with younger children. The water is shallow for at least 100 metres, so it feels very safe for the youngest kids. The Ebeling day-use area close to Brewers Campground has a great large beach. The adjacent play parks are a real bonus, as are a number of additional play structures scattered through both of the camping areas. Be advised there is little shade, so remember to bring your own.

RAINY-DAY ACTIVITIES There is an adjacent golf course and two farmers markets, which run on Friday mornings in Lacombe and Saturday afternoons in Bentley. If you do get rained out, an information board by the concession lists a number of local attractions. Lacombe has Edwardian-style shop fronts, a museum, and a blacksmith. The town of Red Deer offers indoor pools and other attractions such as a farm museum and wildlife park. Sylvan Lake, about thirty minutes away, is home to the Wild Rapids Waterslide Park.

Summary

Due to its location, this is one of Alberta's most popular provincial parks. The expanse of shallow warm water and sandy beaches is undoubtedly a catalyst to its popularity. My only note of caution is this campground can get noisy, especially during the weekends. We visited late in the season when it was quiet, but when researching this book, I found a number of blog comments about the noise problem. This issue may be exacerbated by the lack of vegetation in certain areas of the campground creating an open environment. When we visited, there was a considerable breeze, so we didn't have to worry about bugs; I do not know if I was just lucky or whether the breeze is usually constant.

→ Bow Valley Provincial Park

A lberta Tourism describes the Bow Valley as "A mosaic of open meadows and forests." Established in 1959 where the Bow River meets the Kananaskis River, this provincial park is one of the many within the Kananaskis Country park system and a real favourite among the Calgary camping fraternity. There are five campgrounds in the park: Bow Valley, Willow Rock, Lac des Arc, Bow River, and Three Sisters. By far the nicest is Bow Valley, which is the one that will be reviewed here as the others are either quite close to the Trans-Canada Highway and therefore subject to the noise of constant traffic, or have facilities that are a little rustic. While these other campgrounds make a welcome alternative if Bow Valley is full, Bow Valley really does have the superior facilities, so aim to stay here if possible.

History

Kananskis Country was officially dedicated a protected area over thirty years ago to conserve the wildlife and the sensitive habitat of the region, and as a place Albertans and visitors could experience wilderness.

Location

Located forty-five minutes west of Calgary, this park provides Calgarians with a quick and easy escape from the city. Situated on the banks of the Bow River in the foothills of the Rocky Mountains, the park is accessible from the Trans-Canada Highway. It is also just about a twenty-minute drive from Canmore, which has all services.

Facilities

Bow Valley Campground has 42 unserviced sites and 131 serviced camping spots suitable for every size of recreational vehicle. These well-sheltered spaces run along the south side of the Bow River. Showers, flush and pit toilets, picnic tables, wood (available from the camp store, which also sells groceries, confectionery, camping supplies, and a lot of other stuff), sani-station, and laundry facilities are all available here. The other campgrounds are Bow River (39 unserviced spaces); Three Sisters (36 unserviced spaces); Lac Des Arts (28 unserviced spaces); Elk Flats (group camping); and Willow Rock (124 unserviced and 34 serviced spaces). These other campgrounds are far more open and closer to the Trans-Canada Highway, and consequently noiser.

Recreational Activities

HIKING Hiking is a popular pursuit with a great 5-kilometre trail circling the campground and comprising the Bow Valley Trail, the Elk Flats Trail, and the Moraine Trail. Other walks also exist in the park, and at certain times of the year the wildflowers are wonderful. Try the Flowing Water Trail, a loop adjacent to the Willow Rock Campground, which is good for young kids and has great views. The park has the reputation of being a magnet for wildflower enthusiasts.

CYCLING The Bow Valley Bike Path is a great easy 4-kilometre family biking route leading from the administration building to the campground. For those who want to undertake serious mountain biking, Canmore delivers a great diversity of routes and locations from which mountain bikes can be rented.

FISHING It is possible to fish in the Bow River for rainbow trout, brown trout, and whitefish. Fishing is also available at Gap Lake and Grotto Pond.

BOATING Private operators in the vicinity offer river rafting (you can book these trips in the campground store), and it's possible to canoe and kayak on the river. There are boat and kayak launches in the park. The Kananaskis Whitewater Rafting Company runs trips on the Kananaskis River (kananaskiswhitewaterrafting.com). Windsurfing takes place on Barrier Lake and Lac Des Arts.

WILDLIFE VIEWING The park has deer, elk, bighorn sheep, muskrat, beavers, and bears, to name but a few. The bird life is considerable and includes hawks and golden eagles. There are even hummingbirds near the Boil Springs region of the park.

FAMILY ACTIVITIES During the peak summer months, there are interpretive programs offered that are suitable for every age group. While the campground does not have a sandy beach, there are horseshoes, playgrounds, trails, paved roads for biking, and numerous water-based activities that can be had in the many streams. All these things, in addition to the location being well known as family friendly, means the kids won't be bored.

RAINY-DAY ACTIVITIES With Calgary less than an hour's drive away, if the weather does turn inclement, there are opportunities to head to the city and see what the great indoors has to offer. This is one of the real advantages of this location. Canmore is closer and has a great community centre, Elevation Place, with an aquatics centre, indoor climbing gym, library, and art gallery. Canmore also has a number of shops and restaurants to explore. Banff National Park is just another twenty minutes beyond Canmore.

Summary

The only downside to staying in Bow Valley Provincial Park could be the winds, which are quite strong at times. I recall a time when my son was on my husband's shoulders as the wind howled; he couldn't get enough of it, but the wind was bad enough for us to decide to move on. Another issue that others have mentioned is the sound of the trains. While I love hearing trains and can easily be lulled to sleep by their noise, others complain. Being in the front ranges, this park does boast a longer camping season than many Alberta campgrounds and statistically sees less snow and warmer temperatures than campgrounds at higher altitudes—a statistic that should be treated with caution. We tried to camp here the first week of September in 2014 and could not even drive into the park as the snow was so deep. But if you live in Calgary and want a quick escape, the Bow Valley delivers. And if it does start to rain heavily, or your four-year-old gets sick, or your teenager decides to sulk, it is nice to know home is not far away.

PART 4

Eastern Alberta

→ Writing-on-Stone/Aisinai'pi Provincial Park

Fascinating and beautiful rock formations in Writing-on-Stone Provincial Park.

W hen I was driving the long, straight prairie roads to Writing-on-Stone, I kept thinking, "Is it worth it?" Specializing in campgrounds is not sexy for a travel writer; sometimes I question why I did not decide to become an expert on spa hotels, designer Italian restaurants, or five-star bed and breakfasts. But as soon as I arrived at

Writing-on-Stone, I knew I had hit the mother lode. This really is the place to come if you want to gain an understanding of Canadian First Nations, specifically the Blackfoot and Shoshone, who have inhabited the area for over a thousand years. The area has been populated for well over eight thousand years, but it is the amazing geological formations that characterize this campground and, for me, make it special. The main feature here is the hoodoos, the mushroom-shaped sandstone features formed by frost and rain. These are awesome. This may not be the largest campground, or the most popular, or the most easily accessible, or have the best beaches or clearest waters, but it is unique and therefore should be on everyone's bucket list. Located 256 kilometres southeast of Calgary near the Milk River Valley, this campground is open all year round, so there is no excuse not to visit.

History

The amazing Milk River Valley houses the largest concentration of First Nation petroglyphs (rock carvings) and pictographs (rock paintings) in the North American Great Plains. It is one of the largest areas of protected prairie and serves to both guard the natural environment and preserve the Aboriginal rock carvings and painting. The park is a UNESCO World Heritage Site and protects over fifty petroglyph sites and thousands of works. It was created as a park in 1957, designated an archaeological preserve in 1977, and a national historical site in 2005. In 1887, the North West Mounted Police established an outpost here to curtail cross-border whiskey smuggling. Interpretive boards in the park and an excellent visitor centre facilitate learning the park's history.

Location

Set within the prairie grasslands of southern Alberta about 100 kilometres southeast of Lethbridge and 44 kilometres east of the town of Milk River, this 2.42-hectare park can be found off Highway 501. All services are found in Milk River.

Facilities

Cottonwood trees and willows shade the large sixty-seven camping spots (including three "comfort camping" spots, which sleep up to four people in pre-erected tents). Forty-five spots have power; twenty-one do not. There are pay showers, flush and pit toilets, firewood, and firepits. A small store is open from late May to early September, selling milk, bread, ice, snacks, and some camping supplies. The visitor centre has coffee and a few snacks. Reservations are accepted and strongly advised as the campground operates at capacity during the summer.

Recreational Activities

HIKING Two small trails exist in the park. Battle Scene Trail is less than 1 kilometre long and leads to petroglyphs protected by a steel cage to prevent damage. The Hoodoo Trail is a 2.5-kilometre track leading through spectacular hoodoo landscape. This is a great place for kids to run around and explore, but be warned the summer temperatures can reach an unbearable 45 degrees Celsius. I could not get enough of this trail; steps have been cut into the rock floor and it seems that every few feet a totally new vista reveals itself as the route twists and turns through the hoodoos. Returning was just as much fun as starting off.

A sign warns of migrating snakes in Writing-on-Stone Provincial Park.

CYCLING Paved roads in the campground provide limited

Alberta's Peter Lougheed Provincial Park boasts six vehicle-accessible campgrounds, all of which offer distinct camping experiences. This is the Canyon campground. TREVOR JULIER

Canoe rentals at Peter Lougheed's Interlakes campground. TREVOR JULIER

Peter Lougheed's Interlakes (top), Upper Lake (middle), and Lower Lake (bottom)
campgrounds. TREVOR JULIER

The range of wildlife in Peter Lougheed Provincial Park is impressive and unforgettable.
TREVOR JULIER

Waterton Lakes National Park is much quieter than Jasper and Banff, but it's just as spectacular. TREVOR JULIER

Waterton boasts a number of activities including hiking the Red Rock Canyon (top), boating, and wildlife spotting. TREVOR JULIER

Enjoy lunch at the lakeside Bayshore Inn, rent a canoe at Cameron Lake, and visit the famous Prince of Wales Hotel! TREVOR JULIER

You are never far away from wildlife in Waterton. TREVOR JULIER

Bison roaming and grazing in Waterton. TREVOR JULIER

This is not a sight you see every day—expect the unexpected when camping in Alberta!
TREVOR JULIER

Be prepared for winter-like weather in Alberta, even in the spring and summer months.
TREVOR JULIER

The visitor centre in William A. Switzer Provincial Park offers interpretive programs in the amphitheatre and guided hikes of the surrounding trails. The building houses a real grizzly bear skin and stuffed animals that kids will enjoy learning about.

The Royal Tyrell Museum in Dinosaur Provincial Park contains an amazing array of dinosaur bones and educational activities that are sure to impress parents and kids alike. TREVOR JULIER

Fort Macleod contains a wonderful museum of First Nations heritage, including the Head-Smashed-In Buffalo Jump historic site. TREVOR JULIER

Fort Macleod also contains a fully reconstructed nineteenth-century fort, complete with the traditional musical ride of the North West Mounted Police. TREVOR JULIER

Although they tend to be packed with tourists, Lake Louise (top) and Jasper National Park (bottom) are indeed national treasures. TREVOR JULIER

cycling opportunities, and the adjacent roads outside the campground offer good cycling potential.

BOATING Canoeing is possible on the river, and there are a number of beaches to explore by tube, kayak, or canoe if the weather is not too hot. At the visitor centre, I learned tubes and canoes could be rented from Milk River Raft Tours.

WILDLIFE VIEWING A diverse array of birds frequent the area, including prairie falcons, great horned owls, short-eared owls, cliff swallows, American falcons, ring-necked pheasant, and gray partridge. Animals include gophers, skunks, mule deer, marmots, and bobcats. Rattlesnakes are also in the area; when I visited in early September, signs warned that the snakes were migrating and crossing the roads.

FAMILY ACTIVITIES There is a beautiful soft, sandy beach. In the summer, the water of the river is milky (or even murky) and warm—great for slow

This park's rich history is explored in the visitor centre.

tubing. The visitor centre is fantastic, built in the shape of a traditional tipi, it schedules a number of tours and events in July and August, including storytelling, drumming, dancing, games, and wildlife presentations. The centre runs bus tours to view the petroglyphs and has free Wi-Fi. There is a play park in the day-use area, and a multitude of interpretive boards give the history of the area from First Nations to Mounties to farmers. The night sky is also amazing and well worth staying up for.

RAINY-DAY ACTIVITIES The community of Etzikom has a heritage museum and historical windmill centre, about a thirty-minute drive away. There is also a small museum in Warner. Alternative (although outdoor) pools can be found in Milk River and Foremost. If the weather turns really bad, Lethbridge is just over an hour's drive away.

Summary

I arrived at the visitor centre early one morning as the season was drawing to a close; no one was in the car park. I entered the building to a rhythmic sound and noticed the park official had a sewing machine in front of her and was busy sewing shower curtains for the washrooms. She promptly stopped and enthusiastically explained everything about Writing-on-Stone. It felt more like being welcomed into a good friend's house than entering an Alberta Parks visitor centre. I immediately felt at home and wanted to stay. The best thing about this campground is walking the trails and exploring the landforms in close proximity. This campground is not widely known, but should be. Enjoyment can start prior to arrival, for at certain times of the year you travel through bright yellow canola fields, which stretch as far as the horizon. In the evenings, the setting sun radically changes the colours of the landscape. The only negative thing I heard was that bugs can be an issue (and it can become very hot), but repellent is sold and the campground is shady. Even if you are not a camper, a visit should be on everyone's to-do list. Avoid the crowds (and bugs) and visit in May or September, wander the Hoodoo Trail, and drink in the ambiance. I promise this park will remain in your memory forever.

→ Cypress Hills Inter-Provincial Park

The exterior of the Cypress Hills visitor centre reflects the region's rich cultural history.

Come and see Canada's first and only inter-provincial park, which straddles the Alberta–Saskatchewan border and includes the Fort Walsh National Historical Site of Canada. The location of this park means it has a unique climate that encourages a vegetation of forests, wetlands, and grasslands as the hills in the vicinity climb over 1,468 metres above the surrounding prairies. This is Canada's highest point between the Canadian Rockies and the Labrador Peninsula. But it is not only for these geographical reasons that visits are recommended. Here it is possible to go boating, fishing, riding, swimming, rock climbing, zip-lining, and biking. Alternatively, just hang out at the wonderful beaches. This campground has everything for every age group, and unlike many other campgrounds, it is located within a community—Elkwater. It is impossible to discern where the campground starts and the town stops. There is a different feel to this park and to camping here.

History

The area has been inhabited for more than seven thousands years by First Nations, who were attracted by the herds of bison. In 1875, the North West Mounted Police established a presence in the area. Many years later, in 1951, the government of Alberta established Cypress Hills Provincial Park. In 1989, the governments of Alberta and Saskatchewan signed an agreement committing to co-operating; in 2000, Fort Walsh National Historical site joined and signed the inter-provincial park agreement.

Location

The 40,000-hectare park is located just half an hour's drive off the Trans-Canada Highway via Highway 41, heading south towards the US border. Medicine Hat is the closest town, 70 kilometres away, but the township of Elkwater has all services, including a gas station, restaurants, and a grocery store. As mentioned above, it is inseparable from the campground. Battle Creek runs through the park, which is situated on the wonderful Elkwater Lake.

Facilities

There are seven campgrounds (Elkwater, Lakeview, Old Baldy, Firerock, Ferguson Hill, Beaver Creek, and Lodgepine) offering more than four hundred spaces in the park; an additional fifty are located in smaller adjacent campgrounds, making this the second-largest provincial campground in Alberta (after Aspen). Here, accommodation ranges from sites designed specifically for the largest RV (asphalt pads and power) to basic ones. The ones with no hook-ups tend to be located farther away from the community and are quieter. Power, flush toilets, showers, water, sani-station, campfires, and wood are all available. Reservations are accepted and it is possible to camp throughout the year. The most suitable campsites for families are those at Elkwater as they are close to the lake and township, have play parks, basketball hoops, and hot showers. These are well spaced and offer shade. This is where your kids are sure to meet others.

Recreational Activities

HIKING More than 75 kilometres of hiking trails meander through the park, many of which are also open to cyclists, and bikes can be rented from the township of Elkwater. A number of these paths are easily accessible from the campground. The Trans Canada Trail runs through the park. Amazingly, from certain viewpoints you can see over 100 kilometres, but only on a clear day.

CYCLING The Shoreline Trail (2.4 kilometres one way) is asphalt, so great for strollers or young cyclists. A lot of the smaller trails can be completed in an hour—ideal for young children—but there are also a number of longer trails for older offspring. Trail guides are available online or at the visitor centre.

FISHING If you do not have your own equipment, rods and tackle can be rented at the visitor centre. Try catching walleye, yellow perch, northern pike, brook, rainbow trout, burbot, and common carp in Battle Creek or Reesor Lake, and, of course, in Elkwater Lake.

BOATING Canoes, kayaks, paddle boards, and paddle boats can all be rented. It is possible to waterski on Elkwater Lake, but other lakes and waterways restrict the use of powerboats.

WILDLIFE VIEWING The park website boasts over 250 species of birds, 47 mammal species, as well as reptiles and amphibians. Moose also inhabit the area, and I was told they are often spotted in the campgrounds.

FAMILY ACTIVITIES A total of seven lakes are located within the park; Elkwater is the obvious favourite as it has a huge beach with a cordoned-off swimming area and a playground not far away. There is also a swimming pool in Elkwater should the temperature be too cold (or hot). There is a minigolf course in Elkwater and horseback riding opportunities and tennis are also available. Cypress Hills is a dark sky preserve, the first dark sky preserve in North America, which means evening stargazing can be awesome. Over the summer, a number of programs operate to encourage these and other activities, including a wildlife viewing bus tour and GPS geocache adventures.

RAINY-DAY ACTIVITIES The visitor centre (with gift shop) is jam-packed with things to look at and do. It even has a room specifically for the under-fives. There are stuffed animals, buffalo skins, historical videos, and a fascinating film relaying activities of a wide array of animals captured by a number of night cameras located in the park. The National Historical Site at Fort Walsh illustrates what life was like as a North West Mounted Police Officer in the 1880s and is about 50 kilometres through Cypress Hills Park from Elkwater. An interactive museum with guides in period costumes introduces visitors to this unique site, and there are a number of buildings to explore. Local commercial activities in Elkwood include zip-lining and rock climbing.

Summary

This park feels like it should be in the foothills of the Rockies rather than at the Saskatchewan–Alberta border because of the landscape, trees, and vegetation. The unique environment is easily enough to justify a week-long visit. However, the location (more than 400 kilometres from Calgary) may be a deterrent. If you have friends in other parts of the Prairies, it is an ideal place to meet up. Also for non-campers, there is a wealth of accommodation in Elkwater on offer. These solid-roofed establishments also provide alternatives should the weather be inclement. Sometimes a night in an air-conditioned motel with your own bathroom is just the tonic after a few days camping to set you up for a few more nights under canvas. The only caveat I have to recommending this park is that it is quite urban: while you may be sleeping in a tent, the town and everything it offers is close so the get-away-from-it-all experience is somewhat elusive. But, for the first-timer or for those who have to persuade their kids to go camping, this may be a real bonus. For reluctant teenagers who demand their own space and connections, Cypress Hills is ideal.

→ Dinosaur Provincial Park

Listen for the songbirds singing at the first hint of daylight in Dinosaur Provincial Park.

All kids, and many adults, love dinosaurs, so what better place to take them than Dinosaur Provincial Park? This park is a UNESCO World Heritage Site in the Red Deer Badlands area of Alberta, which is an excellent family location packed with dinosaur fun. The landscape here is unique: a rugged country of erosion with the Red Deer River running through it, featuring amazing rock sculptures known as hoodoos. This landscape is home to scorpions, black widow spiders, and rattlesnakes, so explore in good footwear. But it is not all barren: cottonwood trees offer shade in the campground, and there are large grassy areas to play on and to pitch the tent. We stayed in late June when there were very few visitors, but it was still very hot and the mosquitoes were out. DEET and sunscreen must be the order of the day for July and August. Although the parks staff did say that some years they are mosquito-free, my bites had me doubting this boast.

History

Dinosaur Provincial Park contains one of the richest dinosaur fossil reserves in the world. Over five hundred complete dinosaur skeletons have been found in the park. Seventy-five million years ago, the area was a lush tropical region of swamps and rivers—ideal dinosaur habitat. When the dinosaurs died, their bodies became encased in layers of mud and silt that built up and eventually turned to sedimentary rock, burying the creatures. The Ice Age stripped away and eroded this rock, revealing the dinosaur bones. Erosion has continued, and so now dinosaur bones are sticking up everywhere (almost). The area has been awarded World Heritage Site status for three reasons: because of the dinosaurs, because it contains an extensive tract of badland landscape, and because it is home to a large number of cottonwood trees growing on the banks of the Red Deer River, which also accommodates a large variety of plants and animals.

Location

The park is only 8,600 hectares in area and is 48 kilometres northeast of the town of Brooks, about a two-hour drive from Calgary on Highway 1. The sizeable town of Brooks has all services (including a McDonald's with a play place). Dinosaur Provincial Park is signposted from Brooks and is accessed on paved roads.

Facilities

This campground has everything! There are 124 sites, including 94 that have power access. Spaces are quite open and large, with picnic tables, firepits, and water. There is also comfort camping (pre-erected tents) available. Gravel roads ribbon through the campground, which means everything can get a bit dusty. There are pay showers, a laundry, and firewood is for sale at the lovely on-site store. Reservations are accepted and are strongly recommended. When we stayed, there was a campground host. If Dinosaur is full, try Kinbrook Island Provincial Park (see below), 15 kilometres south of Brooks, which is situated on the warm water of Lake Newell and is an alternative where you can swim. Dinosaur Provincial Park has a service centre where you can purchase supplies, ice cream, ice, wood, and even a cooked breakfast or lunch. It's not too commercial and is a great facility for a camper who is not used to finding such services at a campground. Be warned: it can get very crowded when a busload of local Grade 3 students coincides with the Discover Alberta over-sixty bus tour!

Recreational Activities

HIKING The lovely thing about this park is that the trails are easy, varied, and not that long. You can do them all in a day and still have time left for other activities. Three trails are wheelchair/stroller accessible: the Cottonwood Trail (one hour), which meanders along the Red Deer River and is good for birdwatching; the Prairie Trail (fifteen minutes), near the park's entrance; and the Fossil Hunter's Trail (forty minutes), where the kids can hunt for bones. My favourite is the Badlands Trail (forty-five minutes) as it's so varied and has great views of the hoodoos. Lastly, the Coulee Viewpoint Trail (forty-five minutes) is varied and has good views. Remember to wear strong footwear and take plenty of water.

CYCLING Bikes are prohibited on the trails, but the many roads that ring around the campground make for good kids' cycling.

WILDLIFE VIEWING During our brief stay, we saw rabbits and mule deer. The bird life here is extensive; apparently the cottonwood trees and the underbrush of dogwood, rose, and Saskatoon berry support one of the largest populations of songbirds in Alberta (nuthatches, yellow warblers, and many more). They all like to sing at the first hint of daylight, which is about half past four in the morning in June.

FAMILY ACTIVITIES In addition to the five guided walking trails described above, there are a couple of dinosaur-themed playgrounds to

There's lots to see at the Royal Tyrrell Museum Paleontology Field Station.

keep the kids entertained. The Royal Tyrrell Museum of Paleontology Field Station is also in the park. Here, for a small fee, you can visit the lab where the dinosaur bones are prepared, as well as view large dinosaur bones on display. There is also a theatre that shows a dinosaur film nightly. The centre offers its own kids' activity book for no charge, and it's ideal for kids over the age of seven. One of the most popular events is the two-hour bus tour into the Badlands, led by a parks interpreter. The bus stops on several occasions, and you get out to see dinosaur bones everywhere. I found this to be really amazing, but my three-year-old did get a little bored. Luckily, we were on and off the bus so much that this varied activity kept him distracted. Remember sunscreen and water. These tours fill up early, especially in July and August, but you can book in advance online (DinosuarPark.ca). The field station also offers guided hikes, each over two hours long and designed for older children; one is a fossil safari and the other goes to a Centrosaurus bone bed. All tours and guided hikes can be reserved.

RAINY-DAY ACTIVITIES While the visitor centre at the park is a good shelter from the rain (or heat), a visit to Dinosaur Provincial Park is not complete without another visit—to the dinosaur capital, Drumheller. A two-hour drive away, Drumheller is home to the Royal Tyrrell Museum with dozens of complete dinosaur skeletons, dinosaur bones, interactive displays, and theatres. The town of Drumheller also has the world's largest dinosaur: a 45-metre-long, 26-metre-high Tyrannosaurus Rex. Visitors climb 106 steps up for a view out of his gaping jaw. Now, what kid could resist that? The T. Rex is outside the visitor centre, but there are almost thirty dinosaurs positioned throughout the town. A Styracosaurus stands in front of the drugstore, an Apatosaurus guards the entrance to the IGA supermarket, and there is also a wicked-looking Triceratops near the town's theatre. While some adults may find it all a bit tacky, kids love it.

Summary

To do justice to this provincial park, you need at least a couple of days. Parks literature states that any place seventy-five million years in the making deserves your time. If you do plan a visit, reserve ahead, as the campground and bus tours fill up quickly. Watch the online promotional videos to acquaint yourself. We really enjoyed our stay in early June, which by all accounts is the best time to go. The birdsong in the morning, seeing deer and rabbits on the evening stroll, the smell of the lavender bushes en route to the Badlands Trail, the fantastic array of cactus flowers, and the unique scenery made it a trip we will not forget. However, I have no idea if I would be quite as enthusiastic if I had visited in July, when all the camping spaces were taken and the temperature was at 40 degrees Celsius with no breeze and the mosquitoes in their best biting mood. Residents of Alberta may be used to the heat, but for a coastal BC family making the trip, my advice is to go for June or September. The only other drawback we found was the lack of water-based activities, although there is a creek that runs through the park with a small beach, and it is possible to paddle in the Red Deer River. We did all have fun running through the campground's irrigation system. The sprinklers are turned on in the late afternoon, ensuring the grass stays green, kids get wet, and the mosquitoes keep happy.

→ Kinbrook Island Provincial Park

A very neat oasis retreat from those hot prairie days awaits at this quaint provincial park found on Lake Newell. But it is not only for the cool water and wide beach that this provincial park has gained popularity. Kinbrook is a magnet for birders as the adjacent wetlands provide excellent wildlife-viewing opportunities. Lake Newell is one of the largest and warmest man-made lakes in Alberta and consequently attracts families in search of beachside fun who camp alongside ornithologists enthusiastic to observe the varied feathered populations that frequent the area.

History

Lake Newell is a man-made reservoir south of the city of Brooks. Created in 1914 through the construction of the Bassano Dam, it was named after the irrigation expert T.H. Newell. The lake covers over 66 square metres and adjoins two wetlands, Kinbrook Marsh South and Kinbrook Marsh North. Kinbrook Provincial Park was created in 1951 and consists of a sandy island along the east side of Lake Newell. The area was traditionally a hunting area for bison for the Blackfoot and Crow First Nations. In the late nineteenth century, homesteaders moved in and began to farm the land.

Location

Just about a two-hour drive from Calgary and close to the city of Brooks (12 kilometres away), which has all services, this small 1,100-hectare park is at an elevation of 770 metres. From Cassils Road in Brooks, travel south at Seventh Street East (Highway 873). Continue for 13 kilometres, where there will be signs for the park. It is well signposted from Highway 1 and Brooks.

Facilities

There are 122 large unserviced sites set among a sparsely treed environment and a further 47 with power in this park. Wood is for sale from the most amazing bright-green vending machine, a unique invention I have only ever seen here, but which every park should have. Other less sexy but just as important facilities include showers, firepits, picnic tables, washrooms, laundry, and a sani-station. There is a small store selling basic supplies and reservations are accepted and should be placed early as the location is very popular. Some of the camping spots back onto a large field—great additional playground space. Many of the spaces are quite open with limited opportunities for shade. Campsites A–F are not as open as those in G–H, although they are farther from the beach and day-use area. These sites have a number of grassy areas interspersed between the camping spot itself, which act as great overspill areas for children to run around in and set up games. At the time of writing, this campground was scheduled for renovations.

Recreational Activities

HIKING A 4-kilometre trail meanders through the park with viewing platforms, towers, and viewpoints. The Marsh Trail can be found at campground I and is ideal for children.

CYCLING Paved campsite roads make good but limited cycling roads, so do not expect a good workout. The road to Brooks is straight and not busy. At 12 kilometres long, it is a good alternative for older children who can be coaxed with the incentive of ice cream and fast food outlets in the town.

FISHING Anglers can expect to catch northern pike in the lake, with walleye being stocked in a number of adjacent reservoirs. Information boards list over ten fish species that can be caught.

BOATING Boating really is the main event here. The huge lake offers opportunities for every size of motor and paddle craft, and there are boat launches. Reputed to be a "fast" lake, this is the place for sailing —and windsurfers love it. There is a life jacket loaner station that offers free life vests for kids and a sign that warns, "kids don't float." There are a number of these loaner stations in the larger Alberta Parks. Paddle-boarding is gaining in popularity and is a common sight here.

WILDLIFE WATCHING The area attracts a lot of birders due to its diversified ecology and ecosystem, and spectacular migrations. At certain times of the year, flocks of ducks and white pelicans can be seen. When we stayed, the loons were very noisy; as we drove in, a fox crossed the road.

FAMILY ACTIVITIES The warm water and large beach attract families by the dozen, and this really is the primary activity here. The day-use area and beach are huge, as is the lake, which, as mentioned above, is one of Canada's largest artificial lakes. A divided safe swimming area is on offer for younger children. There is a play park for the kids and fantastic opportunities for stargazing. This can be a really fun nighttime activity for kids, especially the younger ones who are not used to staying up. Encourage them to lie on their backs and stare up at the heavens.

RAINY-DAY ACTIVITIES Dinosaur Provincial Park is only forty-five minutes away and is a great place for kids of every age, but remember to book ahead as the tours get very busy. The Leisure Centre in Brooks has an aquatic centre with a waterslide and wave pool, should the rain decide to pour. Brooks has all services and an older downtown to explore. Just 4 kilometres down the road from Brooks is the Brooks Aqueduct. This huge concrete edifice has a small visitor centre and a number of interpretive boards giving the history of the structure. A trail leads adjacent to the aqueduct, and there is a small play area by the visitor centre.

Summary

We visited in June when the bugs were out in force, but on another occasion we visited in August and did not need bug spray once. There are plans for redevelopment since this park has been operating at capacity for a number of years, so expect changes. A friend of mine, who does not have children, claims the lack of shade here is a big disadvantage, but I think as long as you come prepared and are primarily interested in water-based activities or just having quality time with your family, a great time can be had. On a personal note, Kinbrook does offer the more commercial, developed side of camping; having cut my teeth on camping in BC, I still find the existence of private cottages within the park a bit strange (there are only very few houses here). Overall, though, the park does deliver for those who have young people to entertain and is conveniently located.

→ Whitney Lakes Provincial Park

A small, intimate beach in Whitney Lakes Provincial Park is a nice quiet place to spend downtime with family.

This lake-rich area was formed over ten thousand years ago when the glaciers retreated and formed an area of eskers (long narrow ridges of glacial rock and sand left behind by glaciers) and kettle landforms (hollows and depressions). The provincial park contains four lakes: Whitney, Ross, Laurier, and Borden. It is a great family vacation location and a fantastic place to explore. Alberta Parks promotes this campground as one that will remind you of your own childhood and the happy camping trips that characterized those times, but I think the draw to this campground is that it is suitable for every age group. When I visited, the families were gone and only the more mature RV and tent-trailer campers were around. This is one of the larger campgrounds in Alberta and is spread out, so there are acres to explore. The park is split between Ross and Whitney Lakes, making it feel like two separate campgrounds.

History

This park is relatively new, created in June 1982. The historical Winnipeg Trail, which stretched from Fort Garry in Winnipeg to Fort Edmonton, runs through the park. Sometimes known as the North Victoria or Carlton Trail, it was used in the 1700s by early explorers, trappers, and Aboriginal peoples. It developed as a vital route for rail and freight and was instrumental in the establishment and growth of the new province of Alberta.

Location

The park is located 24 kilometres east of Elk Point on Highway 646. Elk Point is the nearest community and has all services, including gas stations, family restaurants, pizza and burger bars, and a large grocery store. Whitney Lakes is 275 kilometres east of Edmonton, 575 from Calgary, and 120 kilometres north of Vermilion.

Facilities

There are two campgrounds here: Ross Lake and Whitney Lake. Ross Lake has 149 campsites, 82 unserviced and 67 with power. Some are quite open, but others have the benefit of being treed and are quite large and suitable for every size of vehicle. They are divided into six sections A–F, with a few special ones being close to the lake. Each of the alphabetical locations has its own access to the lake and a beach. Whitney Lake has 20 unserviced and 33 serviced sites. These serviced sites are more open and have no shade. The more rustic locations are set among jack pine and aspen trees. Pump and treated tap water, coin-operated showers, picnic tables, firewood, sani-station, and flush and pit toilets are all here. The park is wheelchair accessible and reservations are accepted.

Recreational Activities

HIKING Over 30 kilometres of hiking and biking trails exist, linking the various lakes, travelling along shorelines through forests, and affording wildlife-viewing opportunities. Some trails follow eskers left by melting glaciers and others follow sections of the Winnipeg Trail, which bought settlers from Manitoba to Edmonton. A number of the shorter loops make it easy to hike with younger children, and for those with ambitions to exercise a teenager, day hikes exist.

CYCLING As there is quite a distance between the four lakes, cycling on the paved and gravel roads provides good excursions.

FISHING The four lakes in the park can be fished for yellow perch, northern pike, and walleye (Laurier Lake), and perch and pike (Whitney and Ross Lakes).

BOATING Powerboating and canoeing are permitted on Whitney, Ross and Laurier Lakes, which all have boat launches. Only canoes are permitted on the more remote Borden Lake.

WILDLIFE VIEWING Over 148 species of birds have been recorded in the area. Borden Lake and the bays at the western side of Laurier Lake are the best places to view numerous ducks and geese. The marsh areas are home to wood frogs, muskrats, and mink. The park's wetland and forests of pine, aspen, and birch house moose, beavers, red squirrels, and flying squirrels.

FAMILY ACTIVITIES The primary reason to be here is the beach. Both Whitney and Ross Lake are crystal clear and great for swimming. There is a large accessible beach in the day-use area and other locations, which some claim are the best beaches in Alberta. What more does a family need? Play parks near to the beach add to the enjoyment, as does the good supply of picnic tables and the horseshoe pits. There is little shade on these beaches, and the campground can become very hot.

RAINY-DAY ACTIVITIES Located 13 kilometers south of the community of Elk Point via Highway 646 and well signposted along the route is the Fort George and Buckingham House Provincial Historical Site. This is the site of two trading posts from the 1790s. It has an interpretive centre open from mid-May to Labour Day. Archaeological sites show where the forts once stood, and there are great views. The site teaches visitors about First Nations culture and the subsequent arrival of Europeans and the fur trade. A huge statue of Peter Fidler, a surveyor from the Hudson's Bay Company and founder of the Bucking Fur Trade Fort, provides a fun photo opportunity in Elk Point. The small community of Dewberry, a twenty-minute drive south, has a museum of farming and a collection of farm machinery.

Summary

One Alberta swim guide states, "Ross Lake is among the best beaches in Alberta according to some visitor reports." It was too cold to test the water when I visited, but the birdsong and sound of rustling trees was magical. I visited this campground at the end of the camping season, when school had resumed and temperatures had cooled; it took a while for me to relax and get used to the constant gentle noise of the rustling trees and appreciate that it was not a bear (there are bear notices throughout the park). The location of Whitney Lakes means that the decision to visit involves planning and commitment for many, but if you would like to introduce your children to camping away from the crowds and services, this is the place. Unlike some of the other campgrounds included in this book (e.g., Aspen Beach, Kinbrook Island, Cypress Hills), Whitney provides a true away-from-it-all camping experience and has good beaches, clear water, fishing, and hiking and biking routes. What more does a camper need?

→ Additional Information

BC MAPS

Tourism British Columbia produces a map of the province that details all of the provincial parks and summarizes their facilities. *British Columbia Road Map and Parks Guide* is available from most tourist offices and bookstores. The *British Columbia Road and Recreational Atlas* is an excellent guide of the province, featuring up-to-date colour maps (1:600,000 scale).

BC WEBSITES

Several informative websites give details about camping in BC. For all of the parks listed in this book, the BC Parks website has the most up-to-date information on all of the provincial park campgrounds and can be accessed at bcparks.ca. Make provincial park reservations through discovercamping.ca.

The following websites are useful for travel in BC:

- travel.bc.ca
- fishing.gov.bc.ca
- canadianrockies.com
- britishcolumbia.com
- bcadventure.com
- spacesfornature.org

- gocampingbc.com
- hellobc.com
- bc-camping.com
- env.gov.bc.ca/bcparks
- campingrvbc.com
- travel-british-columbia.com

ALBERTA MAPS

Alberta Parks produces a map of park and protected areas, which is free. It is also possible to download maps from their website, albertaparks.ca.

ALBERTA WEBSITES

Alberta Parks information is available at albertaparks.ca. Reservations can be made at reserve.albertaparks.ca.

The following websites are useful for travel in Alberta:

- travelalberta.com
- hikealberta.com
- canadianrockies.com
- paddlealberta.org
- albertawow.com
- albertacampgroundguide.ca
- mywildalberta.com
- albertacampsites.com
- culture.alberta.ca
- ahla.ca